Kent addresses a crucial need in this day and age - how to help young people (and those who lead them) thrive in the spiritual transition from high school to college and beyond.

Mark Batterson
New York Times best-selling author of *The Circle Maker*
Lead Pastor of National Community Church

I've had the privilege of personally knowing Kent for more than a decade. After having seeing him in family, work and ministry settings, I can honestly say, "He is the real deal!" If authenticity is the new currency of this millennial generation, Kent is beyond wealthy and ready to speak into their most pivotal transitions. I recommend not only his writing to you, but his life and & ministry as well.

Joshua Finley
Lead Pastor of Elim Gospel Church in Lima, NY

The Transition is a must-read for both young adults and those who mentor them! Kent presents the reader with solid, deep truths on how to not only navigate through but thrive in seasons of change and transition. Each chapter tackles crucial issues that our young generation must carry with them into their next season. Kent's clear and powerful prose make these truths easily understandable. Furthermore, the Appendix takes these rich truths and makes them easily applicable. For years I have watched Kent powerfully minister to the young adult in transition. No matter, where you are in your journey, this book will be a blessing!

Just Kendrick
Lead Pastor of City Church
Founder of Holyfire Ministries, New Haven, CT

Kent knows college students. He has observed the transitions of hundreds of students personally and feels deeply the pain and confusion that can touch a Christian student seeking to live out their convictions on a secular campus. He has dedicated his life to enabling these students to successfully bridge that gap both as a college minister and as a Pastor in America's greatest college town Boston. If you care about helping young people to successfully navigate this season of their lives read The Transition.

Michael P. Cavanaugh,
President Elim Bible Institute and College
Founder of BASIC College Ministries

THE TRANSITION

Thriving Spiritually from High School to College & Beyond

KENT MURAWSKI

THE TRANSITION: Thriving Spiritually from High School to College and Beyond

DEDICATION

This book is dedicated to my
Lord, Savior, and Friend, Jesus Christ.
You are the passion and heartbeat of my life.
The greatest pursuit of my life is to know You
and walk with You. It truly is all about You!

CONTENTS

THE TRANSITION

ACKNOWLEDGEMENTS

I would like to thank my wife, Gina. You have stood by me through everything, and you have been my greatest gift this side of heaven. I definitely "married up!" Without your encouragement, support, and courage, I couldn't do half the things I've done (including this book). I love you deeply.

To my children. Kole, Ava, and Jon. You bring so much joy to my life—I love you with all my heart! You are among the greatest gifts I have ever received. I never thought I could love so much and lose so much of me (in a good way).

To my family. Thank you for your love, encouragement and support over the years. To my Dad, Allen; to my Mom, Mary; and to my sisters Gina, Maria, and Kristina (Teeni) Murawski, I truly cherish my relationship with each of you.

I want to thank Pat McKnight and Tony Campolo for being obedient to preach the Gospel to me so many years ago.

To my mentors and those who have invested in me over the years. You called me higher, believed in me, and poured into me in ways that continue to mark my life. Though I am no longer in touch with some of you, you have helped make me who I am: Ron Jutze, Mansel Wells, Michael Mclaughlin, Sean Obergfell, Pat McKnight, Jeff and Colean Hilliker, Adam McCain, Keith O'Neil, Chris and Joan Wood, Bob Weiner, Mike Cavanaugh, Derek Levendusky, Jeff and Nancy Clark, and Bishop Brian Greene.

Friends are a joy and a strength. Life would be bland and dull without comrades. Thank you to David W. Hill, Justin Kendrick, Dave Dotts, and Joshua Finley for believing in me over the years. My life is better because of you.

Books are a collaborative effort. I couldn't have done it without these people whose expertise helped make it better. Thank you to Jason Clement (design), Amy Calkins (initial edit), Allison Armerding (editor), Mike Kim (copywriting and consulting), Adam Mabry (content and theology), Rick Sinclair (content and theology) and Mark Batterson (encouragement and input). Thank you Mark Batterson for your prolific writing, believing in me, and for telling me I have something to say!

Thank you to my church family at The Journey and to all the people who have given me the privilege to lead them (and experiment on them) over the years. I love doing life in Christ together with you. Thank you as well to my Life Transformation Group: Clint Tavares and Joel Travis. Your prayers and encouragement bring life and strengthen me. I love fighting the good fight together.

Books cost money. Thank you to these precious people who funded this project: Daniel and Kersandra Rettig, Barb Zola, Kelly Steinhaus, Sarah Shin, Timothy Stotts, Emma Carroll, John and Rebecca Stoehr, John Decker, Pastor Joe Cyr, Alan and Margaret Travis, David and Chris Funnell, Mary Murawski, Mandee Tafel, Mike Masse, and Carol Donovan. I'm also extremely grateful to our financial partners who have enabled us to be college missionaries and church planters over the last twelve years. Lastly, I want to thank those who were a part of the "launch team" for The Transition helping me to get the word out and making a significant invest of time to read and pull quotes from the book.

Finally, thank you to the high school and college students who will read this book. I believe in you and my pray that it will help you navigate this season of your life with more clarity and passion. May you rise to the occasion and lead us into the next generation!

FOREWORD

Back in 2007, I met Kent Murawski. He was leading a vibrant college ministry that was influencing schools in multiple states. I was getting ready to launch a new church in the heart of Boston. Our early days were filled with prayer and intercession for campuses and universities in Cambridge and Boston. We'd go out on the streets together praying for the sick, sharing the gospel of Jesus, and worshiping on sidewalks next to America's most well-known universities. Kent's zeal for prayer, introducing people to Jesus, and obedience to God's voice challenged me. We were living with a similar God-sized vision and sense of calling. Could anything good come out of Boston's campuses? Could the university be a flashpoint for revival and awakening in our nation? We certainly thought so.

Early on, I realized Kent was not just a passionate enthusiast but a man committed to caring for others and helping people be all they could be in Christ—-particularly young people. This book is exactly about that. It is about God's heart that yearns for relationship with us—-through every transition. It's about God's passion to reveal the glory of who He is to every generation. It's about God's love that never gives up on us. And, it's about knowing how to navigate life's toughest transitions because you've learned one of Kent's best secrets—-abiding in Jesus. It's a book that will shape you, lead you, and guide you—-if you will let it.

In essence, this book carries Kent's DNA–DNA shaped and formed by a God who dramatically rescued him from a life of disillusionment and substance abuse and radically set him apart to carry a message of hope and direction for a generation that struggles with many of the same pains, lies, and entrapments Kent once knew. It's this story, which Kent weaves into the fabric of each chapter, that moves this book from a philosophy of ministry (a powerful one that Kent clearly articulates) to a powerful narrative that life with God is possible—-even on the postmodern, secular campus.

It's this story that makes The Transition feel authentic—-a quality the millennial generation places such a high value upon, and which followers of Jesus were meant to carry. Kent carries it well. He's not afraid to address hard topics, but he does so in a genuine and understanding way––the mark of a man who has learned both from God's Word and from growing up in a post-Christian society.

Having worked with and pastored young people and college students over the last fifteen years, I've seen how many of them are constantly challenged, and at times pushed away from faith, simply because they've never learned to hear God's voice, develop the art of relating to Him, or see the value of staying connected to Christian community. Kent reveals a paradigm that will allow you to experience and know the joy of all three. It's this revelation that will allow the student or the graduate to thrive in any situation or transition.

Kent's paradigm is both intensely practical (it will only work if you do what is suggested) and supernaturally dependent. He articulates the wonder of God's amazing grace while challenging us to go deeper into what that grace provides. The discussion questions and challenges Kent lays out at the end of each chapter make this a book a valuable discipleship tool that should be used by youth leaders, pastors, and campus ministers.

If you are a young person about to begin reading this book, I want you to know Kent is a man who is living what he's preaching (and he's not afraid to tell in the book the places he's come up short!). Allow the practical suggestions and questions Kent has carefully placed into the text to push you into prayer, reflection, and action.

This book was born out of a love God has given Kent for you. What Kent has discovered through his own journey and seasons of transition is that when you allow God to have His way, you meet a God who is better and greater than anything you have hoped for or imagined. My prayer, hope, and belief is that this book will help you to do and experience just that.

Well done, Kent. Keep enjoying being our Dad's kid.

David W. Hill
Lead Pastor, City Church Boston

INTRODUCTION

Transitions are some of the most difficult periods in life and times when people often lose their way. They can be marked by intensity, hardship, instability, and spiritual resistance. I have heard it said that Satan strikes most vehemently at the beginning and at the end of something. Remember Moses and Jesus? The enemy tried to kill them at the beginning of their lives by wiping out all the young children (see Exodus 1:22 and Matthew 2:16). He would like to do the same to us. He seeks to destroy us, discredit us, and take away our potential in Christ. Knowing this, we need to strengthen our foundation, discover some pitfalls we will encounter during transitions, and dig into God's plan for our lives.

In this book, we will tackle one of the major transition times that trips up young people—the transition from high school to college. I included "beyond" in the title because what you do with this transition can affect you for years to come.

This book is meant to help three groups of people:

1. **High school seniors preparing to transition to college.**
2. **College students looking to get back on track or who have become spiritually lost in the maze of college life.**
3. **Parents, pastors, and mentors who lead these young people.**

A Note to Leaders

This book is helpful to parents, mentors, and leaders who desire to help high school and college students to thrive in their faith. Use it as a discipleship tool to help guide them through this important transitory period of life. I have included a note to parents as well as some guidance on how to use this book in a small group setting in the Appendix (see J and K).

My Encouragement to This Generation

The purpose of this book is not so you simply stay Christian in college, although that is the first step. God's plan for you is not just to survive college. He wants you to thrive and flourish in your relationship with Him, to see the world through His eyes, and to tap into the creative power of His Spirit to change the world for the better rather than just maintaining status quo. Gone are the days of simply living with a "full cup" or having just enough; Jesus desires rivers of living water to flow out of you, bringing life to everyone around you through the power of His Spirit (see John 7:37-39 and Ezek. 47).

My prayer is that this book would propel you to leave the one-dimensional mindset of staying Christian in college and embrace a lifestyle of intimacy and fruitfulness. This has always been God's heart for His people (see John 15). You are not just a student or young adult. You are His child and a missionary to those all around you who need Jesus. You have God's DNA inside of you, and He wants you to impact and change the world. He wants His kingdom to come, and His will to be done on earth as it is in heaven (see Matthew 6:10)—through you! Jesus came into the midst of the culture of His day!— Emmanuel, God with us—and lived a lifestyle so radically different and so filled with love, light, truth, and grace that the world was forever changed. Let it be so with your generation. It's time to stop being afraid of the culture and to start penetrating it. You were created for such a time as this (see Esther 4:14)!

This book is meant to be a blueprint showing you how to thrive in your life and relationship with Jesus. It deals with some of the key challenges you will face during this time, as well as some foundational truths you will need to navigate the minefield of college life successfully. Many of these truths have been lived out in my journey with Christ, some of them the hard way. These lessons have come through walking with God for the past twenty years, making mistakes, experiencing victories, persevering through hardship, fostering relationships, enduring times of deep despair, and working with high school and college students over the past two decades. In The Transition, I unpack some very practical and applicable lessons as well as deep spiritual truths to help you succeed. You will learn to:

- **Section 1: Understand how God uses your generation to bring revival**
- **Section 2: Apply the basics of Christianity to flourish in your walk with God**
- **Section 3: Discover your identity in Christ**
- **Section 4: Build and grow healthy relationships that will help you on your spiritual journey**
- **Section 5: Grow in practical wisdom needed for this stage of life**
- **Section 6: Find and fulfill your purpose**

The cry of my heart is that you will enter into this transition with passion, intentionality, and vigor instead of complacency and apathy. God can do so much more with you, through you, and for you than you realize. As a believer in Christ, you have everything you need. You were created for His glory. All things are possible with God, so take up your cross and let's follow Him!

PART 1

FAITH FOR MORE

Stories and testimonies inspire our faith, celebrate what God has done in the past, and give us hope that He can do it again today. In Part 1, I share my story with you (I became a Christian in college) and then share some stories of past moves of God on college campuses to encourage you to believe for the same in your life, among your friends, and on your campus!

CHAPTER 1

MY STORY

College was a time of real searching and hardship for me. I grew up in a mainline church with a very distorted perspective of God. I knew about God, but never learned how to have a relationship with Him—I didn't even know that it was possible. The particular church I attended left me with a bad taste in my mouth for God and organized religion. Church was not a fun or uplifting place to be; from my perspective it was filled with hypocrites. People were not joyful or happy to be there; most seemed as if they were fulfilling a religious obligation to ease the voice of guilt. During my teenage years, my parents literally had to drag me out of bed in order to get me to go to church. I hated it that much! One of the only statements I remember from my weekly religion class was, "Masturbation is a grave sin that will send you to hell."

I did have a couple fun memories from my childhood religious experience. During my fifth-grade class, my teacher made us turn off the lights, light candles, hold hands, and sing a corny church song. As fifth grade boys, we had a riot with that one and spent the whole song trying not to have an outburst of laughter. You know how well it works when you are trying to hold in your laughter!

I also served as an altar boy in my church. Usually there were two altar boys helping, and sometimes it was my best friend, Josh and me. There were countless times when one of us had to leave the altar because we would start laughing uncontrollably. Then, when I was about fourteen or fifteen years old, another friend and I used to go to the Saturday night service because it was short (sometimes less than thirty minutes). We would generally sit in the balcony so as to escape having to participate in the service–that is until the minister caught us playing commando. We would crawl around on the floor on our stomachs laughing and giggling, thinking no one could see us. There was a short wall with a railing at the front of the balcony, and the balcony went up in tiers or steps. One day he called our parents to tell them what we were up to. As it turns out, he could see everything we were doing! Our times of playing commando came to a screeching halt, and we were no longer allowed to go to Saturday night service.

As I entered my college years, I didn't want anything to do with church and religion. During my sophomore year, I decided to try out the "church thing" one more time. There was a gnawing sense of guilt in me that I thought church might alleviate. It was Easter Sunday and I attended a large local church within my denomination. That sealed the deal for me. It was so dry, so boring, and the minister looked so miserable that I vowed never to return again.

College launched me into a three-year journey of misery. On the outside, I was Mr. Party Guy, but on the inside I was dying. It was fun for the first year and a half until one of my best friends from childhood was killed in a car accident. Then life seemed to take a darker turn. I continued to drink heavily, do drugs, engage in immoral relationships, and dabble in occult activities. Shortly after he died, some friends and I went out drinking together. I remember feeling really weird that night. When I got home, I sat in my room looking up at the shotgun hanging on my wall (we were hunters). I thought, *maybe I should just kill myself.* I sat for a few minutes, trembling, and then finally grabbed the shotgun shells, took them downstairs, and threw them out the back door into the woods behind my house. The dark times weren't over though. I plunged into a drug-and-alcohol-induced haze and depression. Many times, I would come back to my dorm after partying and lie on my bed, writhing in pain and listening to Nine Inch Nails, whose dark, techno-like music and twisted lyrics seemed to describe my life to a T.

I continued to try to fill the gaping wounds in my heart with drugs, alcohol, and sex. One time, when I was home over a break, I went out partying with my friends. Afterwards, I tried to sleep until I woke up and saw a friend of mine floating above my bed.

It was probably all the pot I was smoking, occasionally laced with who knows what. But even when I wasn't high, I felt so hazy and out of sorts that it was hard to operate normally. After seeing my floating friend, I freaked out and ran downstairs in the middle of the night. I felt like I was on the verge of losing my mind, so I woke up my sister, Maria, and she sat with me through most of the night. But Maria wasn't doing so well either. One morning over the summer, she confessed to me that she had taken a handful of pills in an attempt to end her life. I immediately called the doctor and took her in. Not too long after that, she had a bad break up with a boyfriend and slit her wrists in a cry for help. She was taken to the to the hospital, where she was in the mental health unit for several weeks.

As I look back, I see that it was during this time that God was drawing me to Himself. One of my daily classes ended a little after noontime each day and every day during that class, I would hear the church bells ringing. They were coming from the little chapel on my campus. I would write poems reminiscent of someone God was drawing to Himself. Here are two of them written in the months leading up to my salvation.

The Tide

> I am crying for Your help day and night,
> Brought about from my sinister fears.
> "Help me!" I say, day after day.
> Yet at the same time I refuse to invite Your help,
> And instead I push it away,
> I try to forget day after day.
> How will I know if You can achieve this task?
> I ask, "Will faith do the deed?"
> Or is it something else; reform or repent?
> Yet day after day I keep it inside,
> Hoping it won't collapse like The Tide.
> (They are ringing for me...)[1]

Confusion

As I walked down that snowy path,
Dark and Alone in mid-January,
Yes, that Snowy path, that desperate path,
It was a path I knew all too well.
One of confusion, one of conviction, one of desecration.
For I have seen this path before,
But it never affected me the way it has as of late.
It riveted my soul, my self, my inner strength.
Try as I might, its wrath I never could escape.
For it gripped my very soul, from the inside
And ripped it to little pieces,
Then laughed as I cried.
Yet it will not inhabit me because I was taught better,
And sometimes I see the usefulness of my tutoring.
Yet sometimes it eludes me and hides,
Like a frightened child clinging to his mother.
But for everything's sake, I resist it and move on.
After all, Salvation must come, Someday!

As you can see from these poems, I was lost, alone, hurting, and holding on to the life I knew by a thread, yet longing for something more. All of this led up to the season of my conversion. That fateful night began the day before Halloween in 1995. My university brought in a married couple who called themselves clairvoyants, defined as one who is "able to see beyond the range of ordinary perception."[2] Call it a "sixth sense" if you will. Really they were just a couple of ghost or demon chasers going all over the world to document different paranormal experiences. During the presentation, they shared the story of a young lady (with pictures) who had "played" the *Ouija Board*, had invited spirits in (which I had done before), and was supposedly attacked that night in her bed by demons who bit, tormented, and scratched her. Ten years later, this would still happen to her on occasion, and her only relief was to run to the church she attended.

The couple made it sound as if, once you had opened this door, these spiritual forces could forcibly enter your life at any time and there was nothing you could do about it. The extent of their spirituality was to use the name of Jesus to drive off evil spirits. They suggested that if you felt negative spiritual forces you should use the name of Jesus and command them to leave. It reminds me of the story in the Bible when some people tried to use the name of Jesus and Paul and the demons said, "I recognize Jesus, I know about Paul, but who are you?" The man who had the evil spirit then jumped on them, overpowered them, and they left naked and wounded (see Acts 19:14-16). A similar experience actually happened to this couple. As they were driving from one of their paranormal experiences, something took over the wheel of their car and they were forced off the road into a ditch. These clairvoyants had a measure of success using the name of Jesus, but still had dangerous incidents happen because they didn't have the true authority of a son or daughter of God.

Needless to say, I left the presentation that night terrified! They had also shared a bit about "the witching hour" which took place from from 3 A.M. to 4 A.M. This is the time when witches, warlocks, and Satanists would gather for to "worship." I prayed I would not be awake during that hour, but when the clock chimed 3 A.M., my eyes were wide open, staring at the ceiling in terror. That was a sleepless night! In the morning, I did the only thing I knew to do at the time. It was all I could do not to run to the chapel on campus so I could cry out to God for help. I did this for about two weeks until God began to answer my prayer. The Lord is close to the brokenhearted; He rescues those whose spirits are crushed (see Psalms 34:18 NLT).

No one was generally in the chapel during the time I frequented it, around 9 A.M. in the morning, but one day, as I was praying, a man with long poker-straight hair, a lazy eye, and a long black trench coat came in and eventually made his way over to me. He introduced himself as Pat, talked with me a little, and asked me some questions. The conversation was pleasant, and after it was over, he invited me to a worship time that he and a few people were having at noon in the chapel. I was a musician myself and was curious what this would look like, so I graciously accepted his invitation. When I arrived, it was he and a few teachers and administrators who gathered once a week to worship the Lord in song. Pat, it turns out, was a campus minister.

We continued our relationship, and shortly after that he invited me to a college conference for "seekers" called, "RSVP." I did not know what a seeker was, but apparently I was one! There, for the first time, I heard and began to perceive the true and simple message of the Gospel or Good News of Jesus Christ: Jesus was born a baby (fully man and fully God), lived a perfect, sinless life, died on the cross for the sin of all humankind, rose from the dead, *and* wanted a relationship with, of all people, me!

I was not born again that day, but I was very touched and began to ponder in wonderment this relationship that I could have with Jesus. I had never imagined God as one who was near and accessible. The view I had always been taught in subtle and unexplainable ways was one of a harsh and angry God who wanted to beat me over the head with a stick when I messed up. Growing up, I heard little about Jesus. Bible passages were read in my hometown church, but I never heard the clear message of the Gospel preached with conviction. Even if I had, I'm not sure I would have been ready or willing to receive it in that place. It was just not believable because there was no passion or conviction. The only sign of devotion I remember seeing was one woman who would raise her hands slightly in worship. After my friend and I were no longer allowed to sit in the balcony due to our commando activities, we sat in the back row of the church. One time, as we were laughing hysterically, she turned to us and said, "God is watching you" (or something like that) and went back to raising her hands. We laughed all the more. I just didn't care about spiritual things at that time.

Shortly after I attended RSVP, Pat invited me to another conference for college students called Jubilee, where around 2,000 college students gathered to worship and find out more about the Lord Jesus. Tony Campolo was speaking at the particular one I attended in February of 1996. He passionately gave testimonies about Jesus and His work in the lives of people. He preached the Gospel with passion and conviction in a way I had never experienced before. It spoke to me in a deep way. When he gave the invitation to respond, I was all in. I repented and fully embraced what Jesus had done on the cross, and began my journey with God.

Over the next few years it was a rocky road, but I knew

something inside of me was different. There were signs of a true conversion. I had a desire to pray, read my Bible, and go to church. I was no longer sour toward life. I began to tell people about Jesus and what He had done in my life. It was real. In fact, the next year I invited my sister Maria (the one who attempted suicide a few times) to Jubilee, and it was really the start of her season of repentance. She put her trust in Jesus several months later and became a firebrand for Jesus. She is now in pastoral ministry with her husband and is a wonderful mother to their children. My growth happened more slowly than I would have thought. Although I had a desire to walk with God, I had no one to show me how, so I continued with one foot in the world and one foot in Christianity. Thank God for His grace!

Although they were gracious and kind, I think I scared the other members of my campus Christian fellowship. My look was different (at the time I wore large stovepipe jeans, hemp accessories, and torn sweaters). I also had different views than many of them. They would usually just stare at me with a blank look when I would say things like, "I think Bob Marley was a prophet." I would sometimes see them on campus while I was carrying a case of beer on my shoulder. I would wave joyously and say hello, only to get a faint hello and an odd stare. Another time we were having a Christian coffeehouse on campus. We had no Christian songs to share so instead we sang some Eric Clapton and Jimi Hendrix songs.

Despite all that, God was working powerfully in my life. One day while I was sitting in a class, God suddenly began to download a message to my heart. This was the first time something like this had ever happened to me. The message was for the people in the Sunday night campus chapel service. I had begun playing guitar as part of the praise and worship team. I asked the pastor if I could share it before worship began. The message the Lord gave me went something like this:

We need to praise God with more enthusiasm. We should be clapping our hands and rejoicing for what

God has done instead of praising Him with mediocrity. So, when we do this song, I want to hear joyous clapping and when it gets to the part that says, "Let all the people say amen," we should be shouting "Amen!" Let's praise God like He deserves instead of with mediocrity.

People seemed to respond in a positive way, and we had a better worship service for the most part. During the sermon, the pastor said, "That was a good exhortation. I hope Kent wasn't referring to me when he was talking about praising God with mediocrity."

I assured him I wasn't and that it was an exhortation for all of us. He seemed to believe me and moved on with the sermon.

Although God was working powerfully in my life, I also had some major baggage to overcome. I had been exposed to pornography when I was twelve years old, and by my college years, I had a full-fledged sexual addiction, which I share more about later in the book. Like many of us, I came from a broken home. My father struggled with alcoholism, and there was constant strife in my home. During my sophomore year in college, my parents were divorced. As soon as I entered college, I dove into drugs, alcohol, sex, and partying. I began drinking and smoking pot almost daily and did a few harder drugs as well, though I never made a habit of them. For some reason I was always scared of the hard drugs (thank God). One time my friends and I did some hallucinogenic mushrooms. Apparently, I popped a few too many. It was one of the worst experiences of my life. At one point during the trip, I remember floating above my body thinking I was going to die. I told God that if He saved me from this I would never do it again. It finally wore off after eight or nine hours, but my mind was always hazy and dull from constantly smoking pot. I would do stupid things like pouring orange juice in my cereal and attempting to screw beverage caps on upside down.

Over the next two years, God dealt with a lot of the baggage in my life. The porn, pot smoking, cigarettes, and drinking, although they became less frequent, continued through college. Over time, I began to experience conviction and the desire for sin started to decrease, but it was hard for me to totally let go.

When I graduated from college, I found a good local church and really began to grow significantly (see Chapter 7, "Rooted and Planted"). In the beginning, church life was difficult for me. I would get bored at what I termed "Christian Kum-ba-ya events," and afterward I would go out to the bar with a few friends outside my church circle. By this point, I would rarely get drunk, but I loved to dance and go out on the town.

The turning point came when I was baptized in or empowered by the Holy Spirit. It happened during a midweek service at my local church (see Chapter 16, "We Need Power"). One week later, I was sitting in a bar with some friends. They happened to be on the dance floor while I was just sitting at a bar stool in the corner having a beer. I suddenly began to experience a sick feeling in my stomach and I said to myself, *what am I doing here? I don't belong here.* I left that night, never to return to my old life and my old ways. For me, the bar scene represented a place of sin and struggle. I had to let it go. From that point on, there was radical change in my life and it marked the beginning of my life in service to the Lord. Shortly afterwards, I began to serve in youth ministry as a worship leader and young adult leader. The Lord had filled me to overflowing and I was hungry for more!

Whatever your background, your story, your sin, your baggage—God is bigger! I know many of you come from broken homes. You have deep hurts that you feel might never be healed, but I'm here to tell you that God is bigger than any problem or hurt you have experienced, and if you let Him, He will use your past for good. If you will throw your life recklessly into His arms, He promises to take care of you. He takes the broken mess we give Him and gives us beauty for ashes (see Isaiah 61).

Many people don't come to Jesus or don't serve Him wholeheartedly because they are afraid they may miss out on something, especially in their college years—as if drinking, partying, and sex could ever substitute for being filled to overflowing by a Living God. I have done both, and I'm here to tell you that life with God is always an infinitely better choice. It's certainly not easy, but what could be more fulfilling than living our lives for the very One who laid down His life for us? I wake up every day with a purpose for my life, to *glorify God in everything I do!* I want God to be the center of everything. I want to love and value people. I have also been called by God to help lead a generation of people, young and old, in the worship and adoration of God! There is nothing like living in the security of a kind and loving Father, and in the purpose of the One who created us to change the world!

Here is one last poem I wrote shortly after my salvation experience.

Saved

Walking through the night lonely and cold,
Not caring about what the future holds.
Thinking how it was when I wouldn't let You in,
Scared but not knowing where else to turn.
How could this be, I once was so strong?
But all of that seems so very long gone.

So where do you turn, where do you go,
So it doesn't bring you down to your knees;
To escape that ever-growing emptiness
To end that ever-growing lonely quest?

There is only One who helped me in my need.
The Ancient of Days lifted me up from despair,
And I eluded Him long until I took His lead.
He took me in His arms and said, "It's OK!"
So I packed up my bags and worked on living His way.

What's Your Story?

So now you have heard my story. Some of you may share a similar story and others not even close. What's your story? Where are you on your walk of faith? Are you spiritually prepared to enter college and young adulthood? Wherever you are I know this – you can thrive in your walk with God through this challenging transition.

Some of you are about to enter college. You've had a great upbringing, a good family who loves you and a positive experience with church. Because of that you feel like you are going to coast through your college experience. Don't be naïve. College is going to test you. Brace yourself, put into practice what you learn in this book, and resolve that no matter what, you are going to love and trust God through it all and help others do the same.

For others, your life has been full of twists and turns like mine was. Maybe you just came to faith in Christ, and you're on fire right now. That's awesome. Stay humble and hungry. Get around like-minded people and strap in for the ride of your life. College can be one of the best, most fruitful times of your life, but you still need to prepare.

Some of you may be on the fence about your faith, Jesus, and religion. You have serious doubts and you're not sure what to do with them. This book is for you. Find some authentic believers to go with you through this book. Seek for answers within the context of a loving community, and whatever you do, *don't isolate yourself.* You are not alone in your doubts. Although doubts are normal, they can sabotage you if not handled properly.

Matt's story is one story of what can happen even with a good upbringing. It was the first year of our church plant near Harvard University when I met Matt. We were having "Church in the Park" as we got ready to launch weekly services. He came with a group of other students from Harvard who were looking for a church and were excited about what we were doing. He stuck around for about a month before he started fading out of our community. I called simply to check up on him and he told me he had found another church. He explained that he was more accustomed to a larger church and so he began looking around. On campus a representative approached him from a particular church in the Boston Area. When I heard the name, I immediately recalled several conversations with other pastors about this church. They had been kicked off several campuses for their heavy-handed tactics. Many people had been wounded and they had some discipleship philosophies and practices that were damaging and destructive. So I set up a meeting with Matt to talk through it with him. When we sat down, I explained to

Matt what I had heard from several long-time, trusted pastors in the city. I recommended several other churches nearby but strongly encouraged him to stay away from that particular one. By the time we were done, Matt was grateful and decided he wanted to stick it out with our church.

Matt's is just one story of many scenarios that can happen at college. He had a good Christian upbringing and wanted to serve Christ in college but was naïve about what was really out there. He ended up sticking with us all four years, became one of our leaders, graduated Harvard at the top of his class, and grew in his faith like crazy.

As you begin your college experience, or prepare yourself for this transition, I hope you will give your spiritual journey the utmost attention. Make it your top priority, because it would be a shame if you succeed academically but not spiritually. *Set the spiritual tone first and the rest will follow.*

"But seek first the kingdom of God and his righteousness, and all these things will be added to you." (Matthew 6:33)

A Word of Encouragement

I came to Christ in my junior year and struggled until I graduated. Content like this was not available to me at the time, and no one told me the things I'm about to share with you in this book. After working with young adults for the past ten-plus years, my heart burns to see you abound through this transition and come out with a red-hot faith.

I wouldn't have written this book if I didn't believe God has so much more for you than you realize. So sit down, strap in, and get ready to dive into what will be an exciting and terrifying journey--faith journeys always are!

Discussion Questions

1. What is your story? Work on your two-minute testimony (your story of coming to faith in Jesus) and be ready to share it next week. And remember, a testimony of being saved at a young age and living well is just as powerful as finding Jesus in the depths of despair! When we break one part of the law, we break it all (see James 2:10). We are all deserving of hell, and we must look at things in light of what Jesus has saved us from!
2. Is there baggage in your life that is hindering you in your walk with God and moving forward in life?
3. What are you most excited about when it comes to college?
4. What is your greatest fear when it comes to college?
5. Have you thought about the spiritual side of this transition?

Meditation Verse

For whoever desires to save his life will lose it, but whoever loses his life for My sake will find it. Matthew 16:25

CHAPTER 2

DO IT AGAIN, LORD

Before we dive into some things that will help you thrive through this challenging life transition, I want to stir up your hunger for what could be. It was during my college years that Jesus Christ captured my heart. In fact, it has been that way for many college students and young people throughout American history. During the 1700's and 1800's, God visited many universities in powerful ways. College students have often been the catalyst for historic change. Since Bible times, by His sovereign grace, God has chosen to use young people to shape and change the world. From David, who was probably sixteen or seventeen when he killed Goliath, to the twelve apostles, most of whom were probably in their late teens or early twenties, God has chosen to capture the zeal of the young to advance His kingdom.

Can He use a handful of radical college students and young adults to change an entire nation? I believe He can. In fact, *change almost always begins with a few.* Think of what happened in the book of Acts. It was a relatively small number of people who carried this description, "These who have turned the world upside down have come here too." (Acts 17:4 NKJV).

I want to begin this chapter and this book by sharing about a few of the key campus revivals that happened early in America's history. You may be surprised to find out about underground church meetings, Bible burnings, and college campuses with no known believers. But through these stories of revival and change, *my prayer is that you will be encouraged to ask God to do it again.*

In the Past

We often become dismayed when looking on the spiritual condition of today's campuses, but conditions were just as bad, if not worse, in America's early years before several revivals shook college campuses and American society. By 1790, after winning the Revolutionary War, America had won its independence, but lost something of her spiritual fervor. Embracing concepts from France, like deism (a movement emphasizing morality but denying the interference of the Creator with the laws of the universe) contributed to the moral and spiritual climate in the American colonies dipping to an all-time low. Things like drunkenness, profanity, and bank robberies became more frequent. It became so bad that women were afraid to go out at night for fear of being assaulted.[1] J. Edwin Orr, in his book, *Journey to the Nations*, gave this description of the universities

A poll taken at Harvard revealed not one believer in the whole student body. At Princeton, where a similar survey showed there to be only two Christians on campus, when the dean opened the Chapel Bible to read, a pack of playing cards fell out, someone having cut a rectangle from each page to fit the deck. Conditions on campus had degenerated to the point that all but five at Princeton were part of the "filthy speech" movement of that day. While students there developed the art of obscene conversation, at Williams College they held a mock communion, and at Dartmouth students put on an "anti-church" play. In New Jersey the radical leader of the deist students led a mob to the Raritan Valley Presbyterian Church where they burned the Bible in a public bonfire. Christians were so few on the average campus and were so intimidated by the non-Christians that they met in secret. They even kept their minutes in code so no one could find out about their clandestine fellowship.[2]

Hampden-Sydney College Revival

Let's take a look back at some of the moves of God that took place in these days, starting with the revival at Hampden-Sydney College, located in Cumberland County, Virginia. There God awoke three young hearts around the turn of the 18th century, and they began to meet quietly in their room for songs, prayer, and Scripture reading. During this time, many other students would gather "as a mob outside the dorm room and, with swearing, ridicule, and threats, demand that the prayer meetings cease."[3] As this continued, it grew so severe that the president, Dr. John Blair Smith, was called to investigate. When he found out why the prayerful students were being tormented, he wept and replied with tears in his eyes, "Oh, is there such a state of things in this college? Then God has come near to us. My dear young friends, you shall be protected."[4] The next prayer meeting was held in his parlor and Dr. Smith was present. Half of the college showed up for the prayer meeting and what was termed a "glorious revival" swept through both the college and the surrounding countryside.[5] Campus revivals rarely if ever remained confined to the college campus. That is why I believe college campuses are a key to winning whole cities, nations, and the world. After all, as renowned scholar Dr. Charles Malik once said, "Change the university and you change the world."[6]

Yale University

Let's move on to Yale University, the birthplace of many revivals over the years. During Timothy Dwight's tenure (grandson of Jonathan Edwards) as the president of Yale, they experienced several moves of God that not only spread to the community, but to other universities as well. For example, in 1802, a spiritual revival occurred that "shook the institution to its center." Out of the 230 students enrolled at Yale, about one-third were powerfully converted and nearly half of those converted went into full-time ministry! Yale experienced twelve similar periods of revival between 1815 and 1841, with the revival of 1831 being very noteworthy, as 900 people in the surrounding community of New Haven were converted as well.[7]

The Haystack Prayer Revival

The famous Haystack Prayer Meeting was a turning point in American history. During its first seven years of existence, Williams College was reported to graduate only five professing Christians,[8] but later became the seedbed for America's first mission's movement! It happened on a "sultry" Saturday in August 1806 when five students gathered together to pray and seek God as they often did twice a week. Thunderclouds broke open, driving them "under" a haystack. Samuel Mills shared his burden to send Christianity abroad and the students prayed that American missions would be spread through the East. Two years later, Mills and few others formed the "Brethren," a society organized to "effect, in the persons of its members, a mission to the heathen." Then in 1810, they convinced the General Association of Congregational Ministers of Massachusetts to form The American Board of Commissioners for Foreign Missions. Finally, two years later, Adoniram Judson, his wife and another missionary couple were commissioned and sent to Calcutta, India, as some of America's first missionaries.[9] *America's first mission's movement was birthed in the heart of five college students who had a habit of coming together to pray! Like other movements in history, it started with a few, not with the masses.*

The Church and the Campus

It seems at some point, the Church abandoned the college campus into the hands of the enemy. Did you know that every college established in colonial America, except the University of Pennsylvania, was founded by some denomination of Christianity? Prior to the Civil War, 1861-1865, a branch of the Church established 92 percent of the 182 colleges and universities![10] Harvard University is the oldest institute of higher learning in America, celebrating its 350th anniversary in 1986! Eight United States Presidents have been educated there, as well as many heads of state from other nations, U.S. senators, and state governors.

Harvard University

I live a short distance from Harvard University. It is amazing to walk around the campus and see the Scriptures on the walls and buildings dedicating Harvard to God. Recently, I took an "official" tour of Harvard with one of the students. During the tour, the only reference to Harvard's godly heritage was that John Harvard, the man the university was named after, was a minister. I thought about playing the antagonist, but decided against it. I simply asked a question, "Can you tell us more about the spiritual heritage of Harvard? You mentioned that John Harvard was a minister, but I see Scriptures and references on the gates and buildings. What does all this mean?" In response, the guide touted off some statement about the religious diversity of Memorial Chapel as a place where all religions are welcomed and practiced, but it was clear that she knew nothing of the Christian/Puritan heritage of her own university. There is a statement that says, "You can't know where you are going until you know where you are from." History provides a window into the future. It seems to me that Harvard's future course would be better discovered if they looked into their past.

Harvard, it turns out, has a rich Christian history, not to be denied. As mentioned, Harvard was named after John Harvard, who was not its founder, but its first benefactor and a well-to-do minister. He bequeathed half of his estate and his whole library to the university. An early brochure said this about Harvard, justifying its existence: "To advance Learning and perpetuate it to Posterity; dreading to leave an illiterate Ministry to the Churches." This motto is carved in concrete on the Johnston gate that surrounds Harvard Yard. In fact, fifteen out of the first seventeen presidents were clergy.[11] Harvard's original seal displayed the motto, "Christi Gloriam" (Glory in Christ), and later "Christo et Ecclesiae" (Christ and the Church) was added around the border.

> This earlier version of the coat of arms, however, contains one difference. If you look closely at the books in the coat of arms, you will see that the top two books are turned facing upward, while the bottom book is overturned. The upward facing books symbolize the truth that is discernible through our five senses; the overturned book symbolizes that which can only be known through the illumination of the Holy Spirit.

By the mid 1800s, the Harvard seal had fallen out of use. When Charles Eliot attained the presidency of Harvard, he wished to reinstate the coat of arms as Harvard's official school seal. This time, however, he made two changes. First, he added the Latin word veritas (truth). Second, he turned all the books facing upwards, denoting the emerging philosophy of humanism.

The idea that all truth is attainable through human efforts is consistent with Ralph Waldo Emerson's teaching on the supremacy of man. As the Concord philosopher once said: "In yourself slumbers the whole of Reason: it is for you to know all."[12]

Although I have no way of corroborating it, the story I have heard states that a upon the Dean's request, part of this quote was to be enshrined on the Emerson Philosophy Building in Harvard Yard. The then-current president covered the building and instead had this carved into the stone above the entrance: "What is man that Thou art mindful of him" (from Psalm 8:2).

Harvard is a difficult place, filled with intellectualism, liberalism, secularism, and radical humanism. Yet I believe God will have His way. This current move will look different than in the past, but God is not to be mocked. Harvard was founded to glorify God, and will speak again. Derek Prince, an internationally recognized Bible teacher and author who went to glory in 2003 prophesied this in 1972:

> Boston is the Jericho of the United States, and the Lord says that when I cause the walls of intellectualism to come tumbling down, then I shall pour out my Spirit upon this whole land.[13]

I believe Harvard is one of the keys to seeing this prophecy fulfilled and a key to revival in the United States and beyond. If it can happen here, it can happen anywhere! Its philosophies have been disseminated far and wide across the United States and the nations. As I was researching this morning, I came across an article stating that Harvard again sits on top as the number-one university in the United States, as rated by the *U.S. News and World Report* college rankings.[14] One could even argue that it's one of the most prestigious, or if not the most prestigious, university in the world.

The Numbers

We may see some parallels between today's colleges and universities and the colleges and universities in the early days of America. College campuses are in poor shape today when considering Christian activity. On an average college campus, less than 5 percent of the students have a relationship with Jesus Christ. During the 2003-2004 school year, 62.8 percent of college ministries in America saw zero to six people come to Christ. You may think, *that's not bad; at least there are a few people coming to Christ.* But Campus Renewal Ministries gives this analogy when assessing the current situation:

> The task is comparable to a man using a teacup to bail water out of a sinking boat, which has sprung a large leak. That person is doing good by getting some water out of the boat, but the boat will sink because it will fill

with water faster than he can bail it out. When success in college ministry is measured in relation to previous successes, it often seems progress is being made when several groups/churches are growing in number. However, when success is measured in relation to the transformation of an overall campus, the results will show that growth in the Body of Christ is not even keeping pace with rising enrollment. As a percentage of the whole campus, many times the Body of Christ is actually declining.[15]

The growth of a few or even several campus ministries is not sufficient for campus transformation.

How is the Church doing at helping high school students who are transitioning into college? Are they thriving in their walk with Jesus? "Most experts believe that 70% of college students who have grown up in church will drop out when they go to college."[16] A group of Christian researchers called *The Barna Group* reported this:

Despite strong levels of spiritual activity during the teen years, most twenty-somethings disengage from active participation in the Christian faith during their young adult years – and often beyond that. In total, six out of ten twenty-something's were involved in a church during their teen years, but have failed to translate that into active spirituality during their early adulthood.

The statistics also tell us that many are not coming back to the Church after college. Even the trend of "coming back to church" once they have children is weakening. Statistics also show that only one-third of twenty-something's with children regularly take them to church. They have different attitudes about church and spirituality than past generations. For example, they "strongly assert that if they cannot find a local church that will help them become more like Christ, then they will find people and groups that will, and connect with them instead of a local church."[17] This is understandable. Christ-likeness should be one of the outcomes of having a church community. Are we too focused on our programs and agendas to actually help people grow in their faith and become more Christ-like? Just for the record, I'm a church-lover not a church-hater, and I'm also the founder and lead pastor of a local church. But I'm not so naïve as to think we are doing everything right. We must get back to the basics of encountering Jesus, loving Him back, loving others, and making disciples. The point is transformation and discipleship, not programs.

Before I go further by sharing some of the research, let me say something: this book was not written based solely on research, although research does shape certain aspects of it. The Lord gave me a burden to write this book and I'm applying over a decade of experience working with teenagers, college students, and young adults. I'm also applying what I've learned in walking with the Lord over the past twenty-plus years. During that time, I have seen many young people disengage from the Church. Although the Church is not God, it is His bride and His body, whom He loves and cherishes. It is inseparable from Him as the Head. Ultimately, this book is meant to help young people thrive in their walk with God, which can't be done apart from the body of Christ. I'm also not supposing that you need to be a part of the traditional body of Christ. Yet at the same time it seems like people are walking away from the Church in record numbers, only to find themselves out on their own. I believe in the local church and believe it can become a place where young people grow in their faith, if we will be what we are meant to be in this hour.

Some newer research from the Barna Group indicates that the problem, is more "nuanced" than was originally thought. In the past, it was thought that seven out of ten people who left high school were walking away from their *faith in Christ*. Instead, the *Barna Group* describes "three distinct patterns of loss: prodigals, nomads, and exiles."

Only one out of nine young people who grow up with a Christian background *loses their faith in Christianity.* After confessing to be a Christian at some point in their past, these *prodigals,* as the article names them, have lost their faith in Christ and Christianity.

The largest group (four out of ten) is the *nomads.* They would still call themselves Christians but are "far less active in church than they were during high school. Nomads have become 'lost' to church participation."

Exiles, or those "who feel lost between the 'church culture' and the society they feel called to influence," feel stuck between two worlds – the comfortable faith of their parents and the life that they believe God has in mind for them. These represent two out of ten.

In the end, the Barna Group says, "Three out of ten young people who grow up with a Christian background stay faithful to church and to faith throughout their transitions from the teen years through their twenties."[18] They found the conclusion of the research to be "that most young people with a Christian background are dropping out of conventional church involvement, not losing their faith." Researcher Ed Stetzer gets even more specific about this trend by saying 70% of young adults between the ages of 23-30 stop attending church regularly for at least one year between the ages of 18-22. Only two-thirds of them return and they do so twice per month or sporadically.[19]

Although this is slightly more encouraging than seven out of ten losing their faith in Christ, it is still indicative of a major problem. Why are young adults disengaging from the Church after high school? I'm certain the Church is not the only entity at fault. *More likely than not, the family, not the Church, is the root of the problem.* Whole books could be and probably have been written on this subject. After all, spiritually vibrant families usually lead to spiritually vibrant children. Though that is not what this book addresses, it does need to be addressed.

How is the Church doing at addressing the specific issues, questions, and concerns of young adults? We can't assume young people are receiving discipleship and training at home, and must seek to engage them at a foundational level. Furthermore, in looking at the research we must ask the question, can one have a vibrant growing relationship with Jesus outside of church involvement? Although we know doing good works and going to church does not prove there is a growing relationship with Jesus, it's impossible to be a vibrant follower of Christ by yourself. By definition, we are part of a body. How can one part of the body say to another part, "I don't need you?" There are many parts but only *one* body (see 1 Corinthians 12:20). As the Barna Group mentions, young people are becoming disconnected in their spiritual journey. The numbers reveal it is nearly 60% that either permanently or for an extended period of time become disconnected from church life after age fifteen, but why?[20]

For too long we've pushed aside the issues that young people have with the Church instead of listening and actively engaging them in their questions, concerns, struggles, and even some of their accurate conclusions about the deficiencies and hypocrisies of the Church. Although I am not going to go into depth about it here, the Barna Research Group gives *Six Reasons Why Young Christians Leave Church:*

1. **Churches seem overprotective.**
2. **Teens' and twentysomethings' experience of Christianity is shallow.**
3. **Church can come across as antagonistic to science.**
4. **Young Christians' church experiences related to sexuality are often simplistic, judgmental.**
5. **They wrestle with the exclusive nature of Christianity.**
6. **The Church feels unfriendly to those who doubt.**[21]

Regardless of whether or not their conclusions about church are right or wrong, young people still need to be engaged on issues relating to spirituality and culture, but many leaders are unwilling to approach them, ignorant about the culture, or unsure how to approach these issues.

The Big Picture

To quote Apollo 13, "Houston, we have a problem."[22] Those graduating from high school are walking away from the traditional church in alarming numbers and many even from their faith. However, history gives us hope and encouragement for the bleak situation on our college campuses and among our young people. I share all these historical examples and statistics in order to stir your faith to believe for a move of God that will shake the earth. Statistics can be a predictor of the future, but they are not the final word. Only God has the final word, and He is waiting for us. Let's not just believe for what happened previously; let's believe God for something even greater. What is our concept of revival? Can God really save a whole generation and turn this nation around for His glory? The answer is yes!

With this rich history, how could it be that the universities have become the territory of the enemy? After all, Jesus told us He would build His Church and the gates of hell would not prevail against it (see Matt. 16:18). We know that Jesus' words never fail and that they are forever established in heaven, so where do we go from here?

Gates, referring to the gates of hell, are meant to keep something out. Gates are a defensive strategy. That means that the Church (the people of God) is meant to be on the offensive, taking ground, bombarding the gates of hell, and we are guaranteed the victory. But it won't be easy. The gates are the part of the fortress that is most heavily guarded and usually a place of great strength. They are also the place where counsels, designs, and schemes are hatched.[23] Right now, in this nation and on the college campus, the Church is not the dominating force. Consider these statistics:[24]

- **North America is one of only two continents on the Earth where Christianity is not growing.**
- **America is the fourth largest unchurched nation in the world.**

It's not been until recently that the number of churches that are opening each year slightly outweighs the number of churches that are closing. According to Ed Stetzer and Warren Bird, 3500 churches are now closing per year and 4000 are starting![25] But this doesn't negate the fact that our nation and our campuses are still in peril. Instead of disengaging from the

Church, we need the new generation God is raising up to reform the Church.

This passage about the Church and the gates of hell implies that we are on the offensive, not cowering in a corner somewhere getting beat up by Satan! Get in the fight! We fight from a place of victory. The victory has already been won; Jesus has made a public spectacle of Satan and totally disarmed him (see Col. 2:11). How then has Satan been able to take so much ground in America, especially on the college campus?

What happened to the days of the Hampden Sydney Revival or the Haystack Prayer Meeting? As Leonard Ravenhill once asked, "Where are the Elijahs of God?" Where are those who are willing, at the cost of radical obedience, to challenge the Baals of our day, take up the offensive against the gates of hell, and take ground for Jesus Christ on the college campus and among this generation? We need a radical generation of world changers who are willing, at the cost of their own lives, to advance the kingdom of God. My prayer is that young people will rise up and be a part of a worldwide move of God to take nations! Jesus told us to "go therefore and make disciples of *all nations*" (see Matthew 28:19). Will we answer the call as Isaiah did and say, "Here am I! Send me" (see Isaiah 6:8). I pray we will.

There are open doors on the college campus today to advance the kingdom of God, but it will come at a cost. It seems as if the only religion that it's politically correct to persecute in America today is Christianity. Your enemies are not professors, administrators, and institutions but principalities and powers (see Ephesians 6:12). A war rages. An assault is coming against Christians in America. It is no different than other times in history. The enemy has taken over the ground of the college campus because we have refused to hold our ground and stand for truth. The nature of Christianity is that it either advances or retreats. There is not middle ground. The enemy knows if he rules the campus, he rules the world. Why do you think there has been such a vehement fight for the college campus?

We have tolerated evil and resigned ourselves over to complacency, waiting for something to happen. The Scripture is clear; the people who know their God shall be strong and do exploits (see Daniel 11:32).

As Leonard Ravenhill once stated, "Where is the Lord God of Elijah? Where He has always been, on the throne! But where are the Elijah's of God?" God is not waiting to move, He's waiting for you!

It's the Little Things

Maybe you're a young person saying, "That's great, Kent, but what can we do right now to thrive in this transition?" For one, you can ask for help. Author and researcher Haydn Shaw shared that just a text message per week during the first semester of college, from someone other than your parent, is enough to cut the rate in half – from 70% that leave the Church down to 35%![26]

Leaders have a responsibility as well. How hard would it be to match each graduating senior with a mentor, other than their parent, who would be willing to connect with them once per week?

Discussion Questions

1. What, specifically, encourages you about the stories of old?
2. Are you wholeheartedly devoted to God, and will do whatever He asks? If not, why not?
3. Do you believe God wants to move to turn your campus, our nation, and the world to Him? What is your concept of revival?
4. As you have read this chapter and prayed, how do you believe God is asking you to personally respond? Who will you contact to be a mentor as you graduate from high school?
5. Will you covenant to go into your college and into the culture and your generation as a missionary for Jesus to bring the kingdom of God wherever you go?
6. Who will you ask to help you through the transition from high school to college or young adulthood? Start thinking and praying about it now and ask the person/mentor to contact you weekly the first year of the transition.

Challenge: Find out the spiritual history of your campus or town. Are there historical "wells of revival" that He wants you to revisit? If not, maybe He wants you to be a part of a new move of God on your campus or in your town. Remember the Haystack Prayer Meeting. Five of you coming together to pray can unleash a flood! The kingdom of God is within you (see Luke 17:21).

Meditation Verse

> Then if My people who are called by My name will humble themselves and pray and seek My face and turn from their wicked ways, I will hear from heaven and will forgive their sins and restore their land. (2 Chronicles 7:14 NLT)

PART 2

WHAT EVERY STUDENT SHOULD KNOW

There are some basic truths that make Christianity, Christianity. If not understood properly, our walk with God can be undermined. But when we do have the right understanding of the gospel, of justification, of sanctification, and of grace, our walk with God takes on a whole new dimension! In this section, you will learn why the gospel is so important, the truth of your position in Christ, how to go about seeing your heart transformed into the image of Christ, and how God provides all you need for every situation through His grace. Grasping and implementing these truths will give you the solid foundation you need to thrive spiritually in your college years.

CHAPTER 3

UNDERSTANDING THE BASICS

As we launch into this topic of transition, we need a basic understanding of two concepts that are foundational to the Christian faith. We will never graduate from these two truths—the gospel and grace. If we don't understand what Christ accomplished through His life, death, and resurrection, we will live lives of frustration and disappointment. If we don't understand grace, we will not experience true and lasting freedom in our Christian walk. On the other hand, if we do understand the gospel, we will live victoriously over sin. If we understand grace, we will have the power to be who He has made us to be and do all that He has called us to do. Both enable us to live a life glorifying to God, full of fruit, purpose, and fulfillment.

The Gospel

Jesus' work on the cross will be magnified forever and ever. He still has the scars in His hands and feet. In heaven, every time we see Jesus, we will notice them. The Scripture says we were not redeemed by mere gold or silver, but by the "precious blood Christ, the sinless, spotless Lamb of God" (1 Peter 1:19 NLT). I have heard it said that we should never tire of John 3:16, "For God loved the world so much that He gave His one and only Son, so that everyone who believes in Him will not perish but have eternal life" (NLT).

The gospel, which means "good news," is simple and powerful. It's so simple it appears foolish to many (see 1

Corinthians 3:19). There are many ways to share it, but it is essentially this:

1. *Jesus was born a human being and yet He was also fully God* (see Colossians 2:9). He was called "Emmanuel" or "God with us." He was God incarnate or God with skin on (see Colossians 2:9, John 1, and Romans 1:3-4).
2. *Jesus never sinned.* He was perfect. In every way, He was tempted as we are, yet without sin or fault. He was the only person ever to live without sin, which uniquely qualified Him to take our place on the cross as the perfect sacrifice (see Hebrews 4:15, Romans 5:8-11 and 1 Peter 1:19 and 2:24).
3. *Jesus died on the cross to pay the penalty for our sin.* He stood in our place, took our punishment, and took God's wrath on our behalf. He "atoned" or made amends for our sin. Because "the life of each creature is in its blood," blood had to be shed to pay for sin. Without the shedding of blood, there is no remission of sin, or release from guilt or penalty (see Leviticus 17:11 NIRV and Hebrews 9:22).
4. *Jesus rose again from the dead* on the third day, conquering sin and death once and for all (see Rom. 14:9; 1 Corinthians 15:3-4, 54-56). If Christ had only died, we would still be dead in our sin. But He didn't just die; He was raised from the dead, snatching the keys of death and Hades and making us right with God. This is imperative to the Christian faith, because without resurrection there is no victory over sin and death. Upon trusting Christ for salvation, we die to self and are raised again to new life in Him! Furthermore, there were over 500 witnesses who saw Him after He had died (see 1 Corinthians 15:6)!

The Gospel can be summed up very easily. It's simple, even foolish sounding, but the bible tells us it is *of first importance* (see 1 Corinthians 15:3-4). We never graduate from the cross and the gospel.

The Intellect

I once had a campus minister (whom I respect) tell me I

shouldn't use a certain gospel tract to witness to the Harvard Community. It was a simple gospel tract that used the Ten Commandments to expose our need for a Savior. This person claimed it was too simple, not intellectual enough, and that it wouldn't work. In response, I told her this:

> "Please understand, I'm not preaching at you, but I never want to overcomplicate the gospel or make it solely an intellectual endeavor. It is *simple and powerful.* Romans 1:16 says, 'For I am not ashamed of the gospel of Christ, for *it* [the Gospel] is the power of God to salvation for everyone who believes, for the Jew first and also for the Greek.' Furthermore, this tract is how we added the first Harvard Student to our team!"

Here's how it went down. One day I took my guitar to the Cambridge Common, a somewhat large park in the middle of Harvard Square. Since the beginning of our journey, the Lord has blessed our worship and used it to bring a kingdom atmosphere. At the time, we didn't have any Harvard students on our team and yet we knew God had given us the promise that *living water would again flow from Harvard.* As I began to worship, the Lord revealed to me that there was a spirit of fear that He wanted to break (see Ephesians 6:12). I took authority over it and then immediately got up and started walking. The Holy Spirit pointed out a young man to me, so I immediately approached him, using the tract to begin a conversation. He just happened to be a freshman looking to connect with a local church! Today we have more Harvard students and my goal is still to preach the gospel simply yet powerfully. The power is not in the presentation; it's in the gospel. The gospel can stand on its own two feet. I don't need to add or take away from it. Obviously, each generation, people group, and culture is responsible to communicate it in a way that is relevant to that specific audience, but in the end it is the gospel, not our presentation that holds the power. Preach the gospel!

I'm not at all pushing aside the importance of things like apologetics (the branch of theology that is concerned with the defense of Christian doctrines[1]) or the need to address intellectual questions. They can be hurdles in the way of someone coming to Christ:-issues like evolution, the reason for suffering, the deity of Christ, the historical factual evidence of the virgin birth, life, death, and resurrection of Christ. These are valid questions that we should address, but in the end, the Gospel is simple; so simple in fact that people stumble upon it. Some can't believe it could be that simple. That could be why the Scripture says, "Not many wise are called" (1 Corinthians 1:26). Worldly wisdom often trips us up from believing in the Gospel. Jesus came to preach the gospel to the poor (see Luke 4:18), and that's my job as well. By that I don't only mean the materially poor, but the poor in spirit as well. It is true that being wealthy, cultured, and educated can create the illusion of self-sufficiency, but one can have the best education and the piles of money and still be poor in spirit. Matthew 5:3 tells us, "Blessed are the poor in spirit for theirs is the kingdom of heaven." You could translate *poor in spirit* as, "those who know they are helpless without God" or "those who know they need God." In order to receive the gospel, we must humble ourselves and come to God on His terms, not ours. There is one way to God and His name is Jesus Christ.

Justification

If you are going to thrive in your Christian walk, these two important terms must be understood: *justification* and *sanctification*. They may seem like complicated theological words, but they really have simple meanings. A lack of understanding regarding what they mean and the difference between them can be detrimental to our growth in Christ.

Many people are caught in the trap of legalism. By definition, legalism is "seeking to achieve forgiveness from God and acceptance by God through obedience to God."[2] In other words, legalists believe that their actions are what cause God to love and forgive them. But the Christian faith doesn't work that way. The word *justified* means to render innocent. When we repent or turn away from our sins, have a change of mind, and acknowledge what Jesus did on the cross on our behalf, God renders us innocent. He takes the perfect sinless record of Jesus, His righteousness or right-standing before God, and transfers it to us. As a friend of mine always says, "God doesn't accept you; He accepts Christ!"

Justification refers to our status or our standing before God. Some people remember the word this way: "Just-as-if-I-never-sinned." In almost every other religion, there is a works-based system, which teaches that if we do enough for God, He will allow us into heaven. You may have heard it this way: "God helps those who help themselves," or "If our good outweighs our bad, then we will make it to heaven." Many Christians have the same belief unknowingly. It's not true. God doesn't help those who help themselves; He helps those who know they *can't* help themselves. We do have to exert effort once we become a Christian, but that effort doesn't earn us heaven. And once Christ saves us, it is a "grace-filled effort," or the empowerment to do God's work through His free gift of grace. The Bible says, "Therefore, since we have been *justified through faith*, we have peace with God through our Lord Jesus Christ" (Romans 5:1 NIV). As Christians, we are justified when we put our faith (belief and trust) in Jesus and what He accomplished by His death and resurrection. This is what He meant when He uttered His last words on the cross: "It is finished" (see John 19:30).

Sanctification

When Jesus uttered those last words and finished His work on the earth, sin and death were defeated. Not only was our salvation purchased through His death and resurrection, but He also paid for our sanctification. Sanctification simply means becoming like Christ and growing in holiness or Christ-likeness. Although justification happens the moment we place our trust in Christ, sanctification is a process. Salvation is a free gift given in an instant; sanctification is part of a life-long discipleship process that will cost us everything. We don't become like Christ overnight. Just as He paid for our justification, He also paid for our sanctification. We are formed into Christ's image over a lifetime, and our sanctification won't be complete until we see Him face to face.

We have no responsibility in the salvation process other than to put our belief and trust in what Christ accomplished. He takes us just the way we are! We don't have to change all our behaviors to come to Him; we only have to come broken and humble. Over time, our sinful desires will change as the Spirit transforms our hearts and molds us into the image of Christ, but it involves Spirit-empowered work. Author C.J. Mahaney says it this way;

> We strive. We fight sin. We study Scripture and pray, even when we don't feel like it. We flee temptation. We press on; we run hard in the pursuit of holiness. And as we become more and more sanctified, the power of the gospel conforms us more and more closely, with ever increasing clarity, to the image of Jesus Christ.[3]

Mahaney also shares this helpful chart explaining the difference between justification and sanctification:

Justification	Sanctification
Being declared righteous	Being made righteous
Our position before God	Our practice before God
Christ's work for us	Christ's work within us
Immediate and complete upon conversion	A lifelong process

"It Is Finished"

These words, spoken by Jesus as He gave up His Spirit, cemented His work: "It is finished" (see John 19:30). Through His life, death, and resurrection, Jesus conquered sin and death and made a way for all humankind to come to God. He provided everything needed for life and godliness (see 2 Peter 1:3). He has done it all—giving us an example of how to live, making a way for us to come to God without shame, giving us the power to live a godly life, and causing our names to be written in the Lamb's book of life. Because of what He *did* we can worship, glorify, and enjoy Him forever. He has done it—fully and completely.

"He who did not spare His own Son, but delivered Him up for us all, how shall He not with Him also freely give us all things?" (Romans 8:32 NKJV) Everything we will ever need has been provided in Christ. Ephesians 1:3 says, "He has blessed us in the heavenly realms with every spiritual blessing in Christ (NIV)." If we are deficient in some area, it is because we haven't had a revelation of this truth. As we embrace our weakness and deficiency and rely on Him, we find our strength in Him. In Christ, we are complete. In Christ, we are fully pleasing. In Christ, God has given us everything we need. He is all-sufficient.

The Grace of God

Grace is the truth I'm probably least versed in, yet need the most. There is a gross misunderstanding of grace in the body of Christ today. Technically, grace is "unmerited favor" or favor we didn't earn. That is the literal translation, but what does that really mean? We pass grace off as a nice little word that Paul used as a beginning and end to most of his letters and throughout the New Testament. But it is much more than that.

I began to come to a greater understanding of grace in late 2004. A friend of mine named Derek Levendusky had a revelation of grace. He calls it his "grace conversion." A grace conversion is, "a life-altering shift of the believer's confidence from self-sufficiency to sufficiency of the grace of God." He goes on to say, "The summary of the experience of those who have discovered God's grace might be as follows: *I will. I can't. He can.*"[4] Derek went through a long dark period of depression, discouragement, and despair and needed to take a sabbatical from ministry for a season. During that time, God showed him his self-reliance and worked this message of grace so deeply into him that it changed him completely. As I had the opportunity to hear him speak and be around him, it began to change my life as well. I have listed some resources from him at the end of the chapter.

For years, I struggled with legalism, thinking my good works earned me favor with God. I would become downcast at my many failures and my answer was to pray harder, fast more, and be more holy, but it just didn't work. That's when God began to give me a deeper understanding of grace. I like to define grace as *the empowerment to be who God has called us to be and do what He has called us to do.* The same grace that saves us is the grace that molds us into the image of Jesus. It frees us from shame and condemnation associated with our poor performance.

God showed me this in a practical way in my prayer life. Intimacy or closeness with Jesus always came somewhat easy for me. But becoming an intercessor (standing in the gap, praying for other people and God's purposes in a persevering way) was always difficult for me. At the beginning of every new year, I would make a commitment to pray persistently about some specific things. Maybe you have done the same. You commit to praying daily for your unsaved family or friends, for your spouse or children, for your sick grandmother, or for God to move on your campus. I would start at the beginning of the new year, but within a week or two my list was out the window and I would end up back in the same place of complacency in intercession. It was the same story with some of my habitual sins I wanted so badly to be rid of. Maybe in the past you have committed to stop doing something, but soon after doing so for a time you fell flat on your face. That was me.

Paul tells us in 1 Thessalonians 5:17 to "Pray without ceasing," but how is that possible? There is another way of praying that old time Pentecostals call "praying through." My own definition of praying through is this: *being in an ongoing state of persistent prayer over a specific issue or issues until you have come the conviction and inner knowing that your prayer has been heard and answered.* In other words, you pray *until* you gain the victory. At that point, your prayer shifts from asking to receiving, from praying to praising. Although God hears you the very moment you pray, sometimes He will wait to answer you so you can learn how to be persistent. That takes faith and faith pleases God— faith like that of Mother Dabney.

In 1925, Mother Dabney and her husband were sent to help pastor a large mission in Philadelphia. As the Lord called her attention to a bad situation in the neighborhood, she asked if God would give them the victory. He said He would and impressed upon her to meet Him at the Schuylkill River at 7:30 the next morning. Mother Dabney was so afraid she would miss her appointment she stayed up all night crocheting! The next morning at the river, the presence of the Lord overshadowed her and here is what she said:

"Lord if you will bless my husband in the place You sent him to establish Your name, if You will break the bonds and destroy the middle wall of partition, if you will give him a church and a congregation — a credit to Your people and all Christendom — I will walk with you for three years in prayer, both day and night. I will meet You every morning at 9 a.m. sharp; You will never have to wait for me; I will be there to greet You. I will stay there all day; I will devote all of my time to You. Furthermore, if You will listen to the voice of my supplication, and break through in that wicked neighborhood and bless my husband, I will fast 72 hours each week for two years. While I am going through the fast, I will not go home to sleep in my bed. I will stay in church, and if I get sleepy, I'll rest on the newspapers and carpet."[5]

She goes on to say, "As soon as I had made a covenant, the heavens opened, and the glory of the Lord fell from heaven all around me. I knew He had prepared me to enter into prayer ministry." Soon after that, the mission became small to hold all the people that were coming. At her husband's request, she began to pray for another place nearby. A man that had been in business for twenty-five years "decided" to rent them his building. But it wasn't all peaches and cream. She wore the flesh off her knees from praying. She fasted. She suffered. Carrying the burden of the Lord in prayer can be a weighty thing, but His grace is greater.

In my own story, I was frustrated with my prayer life and my destructive patterns, but I felt helpless to overcome them. Thankfully, God began working a revelation of grace in me. My story began at a Franciscan retreat center in the hills of Western New York called Mt. Irenaeus. Once or twice a year, I would book a personal retreat there to pray, sometimes fast, and be with Jesus. I highly recommend this for all believers at least once per year. It's worth taking a few days off from your normal schedule to seek the Lord! During that time, I was reading through a book called *The Blueprint,* by Jaeson Ma. In the book, he recounts several stories about miracles that were preceded by prolonged periods of prayer. Something in my spirit began to shift and I started to pray like never before. For hours on end I would pray, read, pray, and read. It went on for three days. When I returned home from the retreat, I didn't have as much time to do that, but the spirit of prayer never left me. Something happened to me. It was grace provided through what Jesus had done on the cross. It turns out, all we have to do is receive it. *Grace doesn't just saves us; it keeps us and gives us the power to be like Jesus.*

Paul used the word *always* on several occasions concerning prayer and thanksgiving (see Ephesians 6:18; Philipians 1:4; Collosians 1:13). *Can this really be done?* I wondered. *Did he really mean **always** as we know it?* Maybe he didn't mean it in the sense that he was praying even while sleeping, preaching, or having a conversation with another person, but certainly in the sense that he maintained a constant state of prayer. In the same way, Jesus lived in a state of perfect unity and connection with the Father. I asked myself, *how did Paul and Jesus achieve such things, and how can I live at that level?* They lived that way through the power of grace provided by the Holy Spirit.

The salvation experience provides a good picture of this. Salvation was a free gift provided by God's grace: "God saved you by His grace when you believed. And you can't take credit for this; it is a gift from God. Salvation is not a reward for the good things we have done, so none of us can boast about it" (Eph. 2:8-9 NLT). We put our faith (belief and trust) in God and He does the saving! We don't do anything to earn it; it's a gift!

Picture a person who approaches you and holds out the keys to a new car (whatever your favorite vehicle is). As he holds out the keys he says, "This car is yours; all you have to do is take the keys." A gift is not a gift unless it is received, so you take the keys (if you're not stupid). Hopefully you don't run around boasting about how much courage, character, and effort it took on your part to take those keys from that generous man. Rather, you should boast about the person who gave you the car. After all, you didn't do anything; you just had faith that he really had bought you a new car, and you took the keys.

This is a picture of how our whole Christian life should look. As my friend Derek says, "The Christian life should be more like a sailboat than a rowboat!" God has provided everything we need through what He accomplished on the cross (see 2 Pet. 1:3; Eph. 1:3). Because we are in Christ, we have access to these gifts (grace). The way we access them is through faith!

In Colossians 2:6, it says, "And now, just as you accepted Christ Jesus as your Lord, you must continue to follow Him" (NLT). How did we accept or receive Christ? By grace through faith (see Eph. 2:8-9). How do we live out being children of the Most High? By grace through faith! How are we going to become holy (a supernatural God-sized endeavor)? By grace through faith! How are we going to pray without ceasing? By grace through faith! How will we do anything associated with the jingdom of God? *By grace through faith!* Picture it this way:

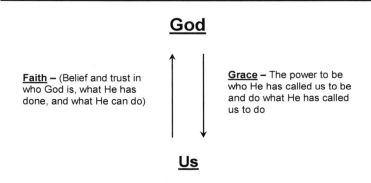

Grace through Faith

God

Faith – (Belief and trust in who God is, what He has done, and what He can do)

Grace – The power to be who He has called us to be and do what He has called us to do

Us

We can't do anything on our own effort. Often what happens is this: We are saved by grace, but then we unknowingly say, "I can take it from here God. I can do holiness. I can stay pure, I can _____ (you fill in the blank)." We quickly find out that a life that begins with God can't be sustained by our own efforts. We have to continue trusting in and relying on God. We must continue receiving His grace by faith and walking in the power of Christ. Paul teaches us in Galatians 3:3 that "The grace that saves us is the same grace that will sanctify us."[6] Romans 5:1-2 says, "Therefore, having been justified by faith, we have peace with God through our Lord Jesus Christ, through whom also we have access *by faith into this grace* in which we stand, and rejoice in hope of the glory of God."

We realize, as we grow in our relationship with God, that we don't need Him less; we need Him more! There are bigger battles to fight, tougher obstacles, and greater ways He wants to use us. It is a journey of dependency, not of becoming independent. We can't access grace (or anything for that matter) without faith. It is impossible to please God without it (see Heb. 11:6). I like to define faith and grace this way:

Faith—Belief and trust in who God is, what He has done, and what He can do

Grace—The power to be who God has called us to be and do what He has called us to do

The Scriptures say we all have been given a "measure of faith" (Romans 12:3). As we extend our faith to God, grace is given by God (as a gift), and we have the power to live victoriously. My life has been much different since I let God begin to teach me about His grace. Before that, I was always frustrated, down on myself, and up and down like a rollercoaster because I could never live up to what I thought was God's expectation of me. I thought I could do Christianity on my own. I was wrong.

Grace Is for the Weak

There is a wonderful freedom in being weak. So many people pride themselves on being strong, but God is with the weak and humble. As we lean on Him in His grace, He will make us *strong in the Lord.* Listen to the wisdom of Paul:

> But he said to me, "My grace is sufficient for you, for my power is made perfect in weakness." Therefore I will boast all the more gladly about my weaknesses, so that Christ's power may rest on me. That is why, for Christ's sake, I delight in weaknesses, in insults, in hardships, in persecutions, in difficulties. *For when I am weak, then I am strong* (2 Corinthians 12:9-10 NIV, italics mine)."

It doesn't make sense to the natural mind. The principle is this: *God delights in our weakness, not our strength.* He already knows we are weak. We were made from dust (see Gen. 2:7). He just wants us to acknowledge it. When we acknowledge it, God is able to come to our aid. It's like He says, "I'm glad you've finally realized that; now let's get to work!" He will let us keep hitting our heads against the wall until we come to this realization. It took me six or seven years before I realized the power of weakness. *Our weakness is the key to unlocking God's power!* God is most glorified when we are dependent on Him. It allows Him to shine. I love what Matthew 5:3 says: "Blessed are the poor in Spirit for theirs is the kingdom of heaven." You could say it this way: "Blessed are those who know they need God or blessed are those who know they are helpless without Him, for theirs is the kingdom of heaven."

So give up trying to do it on your own.

Discussion Questions

1. Is the cross the center of your life and faith?
2. Define justification and sanctification.
3. Have you been trying to "work your way to God?" Please explain:
4. How would you define grace before you read this chapter? How do you define it now?
5. Have you unknowingly said, "I can take it from here, God?"
6. What new truth did you learn about grace by reading this, and how will you implement it?

Recommended Resources

Enoch Walked with God by Derek Levendusky
Discipleship by Grace by Derek Levendusky
In the Grip of His Grace by Max Lucado
The Cross Centered Life by C.J. Mahaney
The Cross of Christ by John Stott

Meditation Verse

But he said to me, "My grace is sufficient for you, for my power is made perfect in weakness." Therefore I will boast all the more gladly about my weaknesses, so that Christ's power may rest on me. (2 Corinthians 12:9 NIV)

CHAPTER 4

ABIDING IN CHRIST

Part I—It's All About Relationship

Since the beginning of my walk with Christ, I have had a desire to be intimately connected with Jesus. I'm not boasting; it is His grace upon my life. Some people, men especially, are scared by the term intimacy. By intimacy I mean closeness, abiding, remaining, staying or dwelling with Jesus on a level you don't experience with anyone else. When I was saved, no one had to tell me to read my Bible, spend time in prayer, or go to church. There was an inherent desire. It is the foundation that God has built in me. God never meant our relationship with Him to be dull, dry, and boring, but rather dynamic, growing, and alive. Few, however, take the time to explore the fullness of their relationship with Jesus, because it takes time.

Many people cannot comprehend how to spend time with an invisible God. In this chapter, I want to explore intimacy with Christ as the building block of our relationship with Him. It's only through abiding and intimacy that we can become like Him and be transformed into His image (see 2 Cor. 3:18). Abiding in Christ suggests that *life is not about doing more for God; it's about knowing God.* As we see and perceive Him, we know and behold Him, and as we behold Him, we become like Him. Secondarily, it's out of that place of relationship and intimacy, that we can do great exploits for God (see Daniel 11:32).

I define success as knowing God and doing His will. In your walk with God, your success as a student, your success in life, and your success as a person, nothing is more important than knowing Him. The bible says, "Let us then with confidence draw near to the throne of grace, that we may receive mercy and find grace to help in time of need" (see Hebrews 4:16). The cross and the blood of Jesus have opened up a way for us to come into the very throne room of God anytime we choose. It's not based on our performance, but on the blood of Jesus. The Father accepts us because of Jesus.

Growing up, I always struggled with the thought that I was mediocre at everything—a jack-of-all-trades, master of none. Basketball was my favorite sport, but I was never the star. In fact, my junior year I was kicked off the basketball team for being mouthy to the coach. After being kicked off the team, I humbled myself and apologized to the coach, but he still didn't let me back on the team that year. I worked hard that summer, and I wrote a letter to an invitation-only basketball camp about my situation. I told them about my passion to play basketball and my change of heart, and they let me in. The following year (my senior year), the coach told me I was the most consistent player on the team, but who wants to hear that at age seventeen? I wanted to be the star!

I was also decent at music and singing, but again I was never the star. I remember going to district choir my junior year. I was a goof-off so I didn't really practice that hard. After hearing the top two male singers, I was glad I didn't! They sounded like Michael Bolton and Yanni! Who can top that? I was also a decent golfer, but never a "Tiger Woods." Yes, I said golf! Then I traded my senior year of golf to play football and tried out for quarterback my first year. What was I thinking? I should have continued with golf instead. Although I played multiple sports like track, football, and baseball, I never won "the gold," so to speak. I was just average. Needless to say, I never reached my childhood goal of being a pro basketball player. Doesn't every young kid dream of something like that? I had a few glory moments, but I wasn't even close to playing Division III college ball, let alone pro ball.

Fast-forward to my junior year of college, when Christ found me. I was a mess, but He chose me anyway. In the following three to four years, as I grew, I began to lead worship and do some preaching. Although they came fairly easily because of God's gifting and calling for my life, I never felt like I really excelled at them. I just felt mediocre. I wasn't down on myself. I just felt that I was "OK" at everything I tried.

Then something changed. When I was 29, my family and I had just moved to Lima, New York (near Rochester), for me to step into the role as the director of Brothers And Sisters In Christ (BASIC). BASIC is a network of local-church-based campus ministries throughout the Northeast. It is an awesome organization that helps churches reach and disciple college students, primarily through equipping students and churches to work together to start campus groups. Over the years, BASIC has developed a network of around thirty or so churches who approach campus ministry with this model. I stepped into it with two years of campus ministry experience and a passion for students, but I felt a little like Moses. I thought, *how do I lead thirty campus ministries when I have only led one?* It wasn't quite as dramatic as the story of Moses, who went from herding sheep in the desert to leading 2-3 million Israelites out of Egypt, but it was dramatic enough for my little life!

I felt overwhelmed. In the midst of feeling lost and alone, I sensed the Lord urging me to take the first hour of my day in the office to seek Him. I was already spending time with Jesus early in the morning at my house, so this was in addition to that. It was difficult at first—especially when looking at all the other things around me that needed to be done. *Is this really the best course? Shouldn't I be "working,"* I thought? One morning, I was spending time with Jesus at the office, worshiping and adoring Him, when suddenly I had an epiphany: *This is where I excel: I excel at being with God! I excel at being intimate with Him, at knowing Jesus!* This was an incredibly freeing moment for me. If there is one thing I want to excel at in my life, I want to excel at knowing God! Like Enoch, I want to walk with God and please Him. For the most part, I now no longer struggle with the "mediocre complex" because I know who I am in Christ. I know how He has created me and who He has created me to be. I am content to be just who He made me.

The great part about the invitation to excel at knowing God is that it's not exclusive. *It's open to every believer!* The ability to excel at being intimate with Jesus is available to every person, no matter how athletic, how good-looking, how talented, or how popular. It's not just for "super saints;" it's for you and me! And if you are going to thrive during this major transition from high school to college and beyond, you had better start getting to know God personally and intimately. It's not just a good idea; it's what God has always desired for the human race: deep abiding intimacy and relationship with Himself!

The Call to Know Him

> Not everyone who calls out to Me, "Lord! Lord!" will enter the Kingdom of Heaven. Only those who actually do the will of My Father in heaven will enter. On judgment day many will say to Me, "Lord! Lord! We prophesied in Your name and cast out demons in Your name and performed many miracles in Your name." But I will reply, *"I never knew you. Get away from Me, you who break God's laws."* (Matthew 7:21-23 NLT)

At first glance, we might be tempted to think this is about performance, because Jesus says; "Only those who actually *do* the will of My Father in heaven will enter." Some may say, "I knew it! We have to *do* something to get to heaven!" But this passage isn't backing up generations of works based religious teaching that told us we have to be good enough to get to heaven. It's by grace as it's always been (see Ephesians 2:8). Only those who *know Him* can find and do His will (desire, pleasure, purpose). Riddle me this: how can we know a person's desires apart from a close personal relationship with him? Unless we can read minds like Professor Xavier from X-Men, we are out of luck! We can't know another person's will and desires apart from them sharing, and people don't usually do that with strangers. *The will must be expressed to be understood.* For those of us who aren't superheroes, there is one way to know a person's will–by knowing them!

God's will is deeper than us simply prophesying, casting out demons, and performing miracles. Those should be by-products of our relationship with Him. This passage is referring to people who *thought* they had a relationship with God, but were really doing these works apart from a relationship with God and apart from His authority. The motives could be many: selfish gain, ambition, pride, deception, a desire for significance and so on. That's why Jesus says, "I never knew you; depart from Me you who break God's laws (or you who practice lawlessness)." So how are prophesying, casting out demons, and working many wonders in His name against His laws? They were doing it at their own bidding. Is that possible? Yes! They weren't doing it because Jesus willed or desired it but rather for self-glorification. They went against the higher law of love—"Love the Lord your God with all your heart, soul, mind and strength and love your neighbor as yourself" (Mark 12:30-31).

Without a love relationship with Jesus, everything else is for naught. Without this, all our good deeds are for vain human glory. Without relationship, we can preach, pray, fast, heal the sick, or raise the dead, but it won't matter. These people to whom Jesus will say, "Depart from Me, I never knew you," are those who think their good works are enough to get them into heaven. It's the ultimate deception. It's a performance-based system. It's legalism and it doesn't work. The only thing that allows us to enter His kingdom is relationship with Him (see Matthew 7:23; 25:12; Luke 13:27; John 3:3, 8:19; 10:14). His blood, not our good works, is what takes away sin. *Without the shedding of blood, there is no forgiveness* (see Hebrews 9:22 NLT). The Bible goes on to say:

For this is My [Jesus'] blood of the new covenant, which is shed for many *for the remission (pardon) of sins.* (Matthew 26:28 NKJV, commentary and italics mine)

Blessed are those whose lawless deeds are forgiven, and whose sins are covered. (Romans 4:7 ESV)

We can take a deep breath; it's not dependent on us! We don't have to work more, pray more, give more, or climb the corporate ladder of Christianity any longer. Jesus paid it all, and as long as we put your full trust in Him, His atoning work on the cross, and His resurrection, we are justified–rendered innocent of our sins and put into right relationship with Him. Being saved from our sin and starting a relationship with Jesus is free, but becoming a disciple will cost you everything! Walking with Jesus is all about a relationship that's been purchased through the cross. It has been about relationship since the very beginning (see Genesis 3:8-9). Remember when Jesus taught His disciples to pray? Almost everyone knows or has heard the Lord's Prayer (see Matthew 6:9-13). He starts off with, *"Our Father who is in heaven."* It starts with relationship. Without relationships, with both God and other people, life is empty and meaningless.

Some incredible saints of old had the same desire for intimacy with God. Think of Daniel, who three times a day would bow toward Jerusalem in prayer to God. It wasn't a legalistic expression of obedience; it was the outward expression of an inward cry to know God, "...but the people who know their God shall prove themselves strong and shall stand firm and do exploits [for God]" (Daniel 11:32 NASB). Paul was another whose desire to know Christ trumped every other desire. "For I determined to know nothing among you except Jesus Christ, and Him crucified" (1 Corinthians 2:2).

Regardless of the field God calls you into–business, arts and entertainment, sports, education, politics, or vocational ministry–*your higher calling is to know Him.* How can we become like someone we do not know? How can we please someone unless we know what pleases them? How can we be changed into His image if we don't know what He looks like? It's impossible. Knowing Him is our highest calling, period.

Abiding

John 15:1-8 is probably the greatest passage in the Bible on this subject. In this short passage, Jesus teaches us a powerful truth: *lasting fruit comes from lasting relationship.* As we grow in our relationship with Jesus, we realize that life is more about knowing God and less about doing for God. Any eternal fruit that comes from our lives—and God desires lots of it—is going to come from our relationship with God. I've heard it said that we are to live *from* God not *for* God. It's when we know Him that He reveals His will to us. When we know His will, we can act on it and produce fruit that remains. What is fruit? In the words of author Bruce Wilkinson, "Fruit represents good works—a thought, attitude, or action of ours that God values because it glorifies Him."[1]

By far the best resource I have ever read about abiding in Christ is Bruce Wilkinson's *Secrets of the Vine* based on John 15. I highly recommend that you read it. It's one of those short books that is packed with rich spiritual truth and power.

Here are six truths or "secrets" mined from John 15:1-8 that will help you as you learn to abide in Christ.

Jesus Is The True Vine

In John 15:1, Jesus says, "I am the true vine and my Father is the vinedresser (or gardener)." If there is a *true* vine, there must also be *false* vines or Jesus wouldn't say it. Through the vine comes nourishment to the branches. In my experience, we can either draw nourishment from Christ and that which He ordains for our lives (the true vine) or we draw nourishment from apart from Christ and that which He ordains (false vines). Some examples of false vines could be: unwholesome music, entertainment and media, or relationships that hinder us rather than help us. Here is a question you can ask to determine whether something is a false vine: is this bringing me closer to Christ and making me more like Christ?

> Carefully determine what pleases the Lord. Take no part in the worthless deeds of evil and darkness; instead, expose them. It is shameful even to talk about the things that ungodly people do in secret. (Ephesians 5:10-12 NLT)

God Is The Gardener

John 15:1 calls Father God the Vinedresser or Gardener. In other words, it's His job to take care of the plants and make sure they bear fruit. If your life consistently bears no fruit or some fruit, the Gardener will intervene either through discipline or pruning. Lets talk about discipline first.

Discipline is almost always the result of sin. In John 15:2, Jesus establishes this principle when He says, "Every branch of mine that does not bear fruit He takes away." When you study out the verse, you find that "lifts up" is a better translation than "takes away." God is a good Gardener and we are His branches. He won't allow our lives to be fruitless so when He sees that, He will intervene through discipline.

In his book, Bruce Wilkinson shares some insights that came from sitting down with a man who owned a large vineyard. The man said:

> "New branches have a natural tendency to trail down and grow along the ground, but they don't bear fruit down there. When branches grow along the ground, the leaves get coated in dust. When it rains, they get muddy and mildewed. The branch becomes sick and useless."

Bruce assumed you throw the branch away when it gets like that, but the vinedresser said, "Oh no! the branch is much to valuable for that. We go through the vineyard with a bucket of water looking for those branches. We lift them up and wash them off. Then we wrap them around the trellis or tie them up. Pretty soon they're thriving."[2] So instead of getting rid of us, God lifts us up, cleans us off and ties us to the trellis, putting us on our way to bearing fruit–if we respond to His discipline that is (see Hebrews 12:5-11). The answer is to repent.

The other form of intervention God uses is pruning. Pruning is the cutting off of unproductive things that are hindering us from producing maximum fruit. Discipline comes as the result of sin whereas pruning comes when we are doing something right. Our lives are bearing *some* fruit, but God wants them to bear *abundant* fruit. Sometimes it's hard to tell the difference because they are both painful. To determine whether your pain comes from discipline or pruning, you must look at your level of fruit. Is your life bearing no fruit or some fruit?

Bruce Wilkinson recommends asking God directly, "Do I have a major sin that's causing You to discipline me?" If He doesn't answer you in one week, then take it by faith that it's pruning!"[3]

Our Highest Calling Is To Abide

Abiding in and knowing Jesus is arguably one of the most important things, if not the most important thing, in Scripture. Think of it this way. If we don't abide, we can produce no fruit and God gets no glory, and giving God glory is the very reason we were created (see Isaiah 43:7)! Some may say obedience is even more important, but if we don't know God's will and desire, how can we truly obey? We can only know His will by remaining in Christ and His word.

Abide is actually a verb from the Greek word, *mĕnō,* which means to stay, continue, dwell, endure, be present, and remain.[4] Jesus can't make us abide; it's something we have to learn to do. It can be hard for those of us who are doers until we realize things that yield eternal lasting fruit only come from abiding.

Here is a questions we must ask ourselves: *how much of what we are doing came from abiding in Jesus and is bearing eternal fruit?* Let the words of Jesus sink in: "Whoever abides in me and I in him, he it is that bears much fruit, for apart from me you can do nothing" (John 15:5).

A Branch That Doesn't Abide Is Dying

It's simple – a branch that isn't connected to the vine is dying. As on any tree, in order to live and bear fruit, the branch must be connected to the vine.

> If anyone does not abide in me he is thrown away like a branch and withers; and the branches are gathered, thrown into the fire, and burned. (John 15:6)

I don't believe this verse is threatening us with hell. A branch's job is to stay connected to the vine and bear fruit. That's what branches do. If not connected to the vine, they will wither up, fall off, and have no better purpose than firewood! In Scripture, the fire of God can refer to several different things, including passion, purity, or trials. In this case, I believe it's referring to trials. Think of it this way, *when we are out of the will of God (abiding and producing fruit), we welcome the fire of God.* In other words, God turns up the intensity in order to get our attention and connect us to the vine. We already discussed how God the Father lifts up every branch *in Him* that does not bear fruit. God would never throw away a branch just because it's not producing fruit, but rather, He will do whatever it takes to get it back in connection with the vine so it can start producing fruit.

Abiding Brings the Blessing of God

> If you abide in me, and my words abide in you, ask whatever you wish, and it will be done for you. (John 15:7)

If is a conditional word: *if you abide in Me.* That means we can choose to abide or not abide in Christ and His word. If we do–blessings and fruit will abound. When we know Christ and understand His will, His desires become ours. When we pray, we will be asking for the things that please His heart, and thus it will be done for us. Answered prayers are fruit that bring God glory!

Earlier in the chapter, I shared my story about discovering

what I was good at or finding my niche. I excel at knowing God, but I want to share the rest of the story with you. As I began spending an hour per day with the Lord at my office, things began to happen. Ministry started moving forward. I began receiving calls from people I had been trying to reach for months (pastors aren't always easy to get a hold of). Plans and strategies became clear on how to take the next steps in the ministry I was leading. The ministry grew and became healthy again. When I became the director, it had been maintaining the status quo due to a long period without an on-site director. I don't taking credit for turning things around; it was God through me. I had no idea how to move things forward, but God did!

The Final Result – God's Glory

What comes as a result of abiding in Christ? We produce fruit, proving that we are His disciples and glorify God. God's glory is the ultimate goal.

> By this my Father is glorified, that you bear much fruit and so prove to be my disciples. (John 15:8)

Through abiding in Christ, our highest purpose is fulfilled. This is what we were created to do – bring God glory. Listen how God said it through Isaiah:

> Everyone who is called by my name, *whom I have created for my glory,* I have formed him, ye, I have made him. (Isaiah 43:7, italics mine)

Regardless of what vocation we do, how much money we make or don't make, or our station in life, this is the overarching purpose of our lives. This is what disciples do—produce lots of fruit and glorify God. We ought to be supremely interested in God's glory. *Only things done for His glory will last for eternity.* C.T. Studd said it this way in His famous poem: "Only one life, 'twill soon be past, only what's done for Christ will last."

God's glory is little understood. What does it mean to live for His glory? Pastor and author John Piper defines God's glory this way:

> I believe the glory of God is the going public of His infinite worth. I define the holiness of God as the infinite value of God, the infinite intrinsic worth of God.[5]

How do we give Him glory by going public with His infinite worth? "Let your light shine before others, so that they may see your good works and give *glory* to your Father who is in heaven" (Matthew 5:16, italics mine).

When we let our light shine, when we love one another the way He loved us, Habukkuk 2:14 will comes to pass: "For the earth will be filled with the knowledge of the glory of the LORD as the waters cover the sea."

Resources

Appendix A: Plan for Devoted Time
Secrets of the Vine by Bruce Wilkinson
Secrets of the Secret Place by Bob Sorge

Meditation Verse

> I am the vine; you are the branches. If a man remains in me and I in him, he will bear much fruit; apart from me you can do nothing. (John 15:5 NIV)

PART 3

IDENTITY: THE MOST IMPORTANT THING ABOUT YOU

We all long to know who we are, but the things by which we define ourselves are often lesser than the things by which God defines us. We use words like mother, father, teacher, pastor, student, man, or woman to define our identity, but those all pale in comparison to our true identity as children of God. In this section, we explore what the Bible says about who God is and who we are in His Son, Jesus Christ. Learning your true identity will shape the way you relate to God and to others, and help you navigate your college years with clarity and certainty.

CHAPTER 5

IDENTITY PART 1: THE FATHER HEART OF GOD

God has always been interested in a relationship with His children. Even when Jesus taught His disciples to pray, the first words of the prayer were, *"Our Father,* who is in heaven..." (Matthew 6:9, italics mine).

Knowing God in Order to Know Ourselves

One of the most important ways we need to know God is as *Father.* A father (or lack of) is probably the most significant person in the forming of a person's identity. Fathers establish identity. They define.

In the story called "Wasted Day," (an excerpt from the book *To a Child Love is Spelled T-I-M-E: What a Child Really Needs From You)* authors Mac Anderson and Lance Wubbels highlight the importance of fathers. As a father is digging through some old pictures and journals, longing for the memories of his deceased wife, he comes across his son's six-year-old journal. He soon finds out that his son's recollection of those days was far different than his own. He goes to an old cabinet to find his journal and compare the two. Here is a quote from the story,

> As he opened his journal, the old man's eyes fell upon an inscription that stood out because it was so brief in

comparison to other days. In his own neat handwriting there were these words:

Wasted the whole day fishing with Jimmy. Didn't catch a thing.

With a deep sigh and a shaking hand, he took Jimmy's journal and found the boy's entry for the same day, June 4. Large scrawling letters, pressed deeply into the paper, read:

Went fishing with my dad. Best day of my life.[1]

A wound like this is hard to overcome and can cripple a child for life. Fathers sometimes don't realize the weight their words and actions carry.

My own family experience was deeply flawed. Though I no longer blame my parents, and I know they did the best they could, there was a lot of pain and hurt to overcome from family discord and divorce. Along the way, many of my father's struggles became my own, but God has been faithful to heal each and every one of them. He also restored my relationship with my Dad, and I had the privilege of leading him to Christ several years ago. Today we have a good relationship for which I am thankful.

The reality is that 50-60 percent of the younger generation comes from broken homes. Look at these modern statistics concerning fathers:

- 90 percent of homeless and runaway children are from fatherless homes.
- 71 percent of pregnant teenagers lack a father.
- 63 percent of youth suicides are from fatherless homes.
- 71 percent of high school dropouts come from fatherless homes.

- 70 percent of juveniles in state operated institutions have no father.
- 85 percent of youths in prisons grew up in a fatherless home.[2]

According to the Scriptures, fatherlessness comes with a curse (see Malachi 4:5-6). That's easy to see from these statistics.

A number of years ago, I was sharing about the Father heart of God at a meeting of college students at the University of Buffalo. During the meeting, I shared part of my testimony. Afterward, a young man who I had never met before came up to me and began to share with me about part of my future calling. He said, "Your testimony is so powerful. I believe God is going to use you to break the curse of fatherlessness off a generation." But it's not just me who will do this. There will be many! Malachi the prophet foretells as much,

> Behold, I will send you Elijah the prophet before the great and awesome day of the LORD comes. And he will turn the hearts of fathers to their children and the hearts of children to their fathers, lest I come and strike the land with a decree of utter destruction. (Malachi 4:5-6)

I'm not claiming to be Elijah, but I do believe many will be empowered with part of the same calling Elijah had–to turn the hearts of fathers to their children and the hearts of children to their fathers. This would include spiritual fathers. God wants to break the curse of fatherlessness off this generation. He longs to embrace this generation with His tangible Father's love! So many people have a distorted view of fathers, but the Bible says God is the perfect heavenly Father (see Matthew 5:48).

His Plan from the Beginning

God the Father has always desired intimacy and relationship with His children. This has ever been the plan. God is not an absent Father. Adam and Eve chose to separate themselves from Him:

> They heard the sound of the LORD God walking in the garden in the cool of the day, and the man and his wife hid themselves from the presence of the LORD God among the trees of the garden. Then the LORD God called to the man, and said to him, "Where are you?" (Genesis 3:8-9 NASB)

Sin separated humankind from their Father and Creator, God. Jesus, the second Adam, has restored our ability to come into the Father's presence anytime, anyplace (see Matthew 27:51; Hebrews 10:16-22).

We need to begin to view the Father rightly. More often than not, we view our heavenly Father through the lens of our earthly fathers. If we have a negative view of fathers, it skews our view of a perfect God. In order to change that, we have to see Him rightly as He gives us revelation of Himself. The Word of God must shape our view of Him and penetrate our hearts. As we do this, things will begin to come clear. It's necessary to look from God to man, not from man to God. As John Piper has said, when we look at man to understand God, we will skew Him badly.

God began to restore me and give me a right view of Him shortly after my salvation. That night is still vivid in my mind. I was praying with my youth pastor one hot summer August night just before the start of youth camp. As we were praying, I had a profound experience with Abba that I will never forget. In that time of prayer, God spoke to my heart so clearly. As I sat there under the stars in utter amazement, He said these simple but profound words, "I'm proud of you son." This may not seem like a big deal to you, but it was a game-changer for me. That night marked me and defined me. For the first time, I knew what it meant to be His son, and the identity and acceptance that go with that. He wants to mark you as well. He did the same thing with His Son, Jesus:

> After Jesus was baptized by John, the Father spoke over Him; "And suddenly a voice came from heaven, saying, "This is My beloved Son, in whom I am well pleased." (see Matthew 3:17)

He didn't say that because Jesus had performed a miracle or did good deed, but just because of who He is. Because He is pleased with His perfect Son, if you are "in Christ," God is pleased with you as well. Jesus' perfection covers your imperfection. He loves you because He loves you–not for what you can do for Him but because of who you are in Him. Your significance can never come from your performance; it can only come through your identity as a child of God. That's why it's a mistake to try to relate to God by your performance (a worker) rather than by your position (a son or daughter).

Why not stop right now and take a few minutes to let Abba Father speak over you and hear what He has to say to you? If you will open up your heart to Him, He will speak His approval over you. He is longing to do this. If you've never come to Him through Jesus, His Son, that's the first step. God has been waiting for you to come to Him so He can mark you and establish your identity as His son or daughter. He wants to claim you, even if no one else does. He loves you for you. He wants to scoop you up into His arms and toss you in the air. He wants to pull you up into His lap, hold you, and smother you with kisses.

Go ahead, do it right now. Draw close to Him.

Now, what did He speak to you? Write it down! Meditate on it. Hang it up on your wall. If you don't have a journal, now is a good time to start one.

It's not possible to find our identity apart from our Father and Creator. Since we are *created* beings, our Creator has put Himself into us, and we will never find out who we are apart from Him. He longs to reveal Himself to us as Father. Once you know Him as Father, and you understand who you are in Him, you will begin to love and serve others selflessly:

> Jesus knew that the Father had put all things under his power, and that he had come from God and was returning to God; so he got up from the meal, took off his outer clothing, and wrapped a towel around his waist. After that, he poured water into a basin and began to wash his disciples' feet, drying them with the towel that was wrapped around him. (John 13:3-5 NIV)

What Is Your Real Name?

A while back, I was reading a John Eldredge book called *Waking the Dead*. In the book, he encourages readers to ask God your real name—to ask God, *who am I to You?* Although "Son" or "Daughter" is first and foremost, He also speaks His purpose over us through names.

It could be the name your parents gave you. I am big on the meaning of names. My son's name is Kole, which means "victory of the people." We constantly speak over him that he is going to lead people into victory in Jesus. My daughter's name is Ava, meaning, "filled with life." We consistently speak over her that she is filled with the abundant life of God and wherever she goes there will be life. My youngest son's name is Jon. He was named after John the Baptist and we believe He has a prophetic call upon His life. My name is Kent, which means "handsome" (no spiritual relevance, just thought you might like to know).

One day, as Eldredge's book recommended, I was asking God, "What is my real name? Who am I to you?" The Lord said, "You are My Elijah!" This carries with it a lot of significance for me, because I feel part of my calling in life, like Elijah, is to "turn the hearts of the fathers to their children and the hearts of children to their fathers" (Malachi 4:5-6). A few years earlier, He had spoken to me, saying, "Remember the name Elijah. Like

Elijah, you are going to do great and mighty things for Me, but you are going to raise up many Elishas who go on to do greater things than you!"

Go ahead, ask Daddy God, "What is my real name? Who am I to you?" It will change your life!

He Is Fully Pleased With You

Did you know, in Christ, you are fully pleasing to God – right now?

> And so, from the day we heard, we have not ceased to pray for you, asking that you may be filled with the knowledge of his will in all spiritual wisdom and understanding, so as to walk in a manner worthy of the Lord, *fully pleasing to him,* bearing fruit in every good work and increasing in the knowledge of God. (Colossians 1:9-10, italics mine)

Since we know that salvation is not based on works (see Ephesians 2:8-9), and that we have been justified (rendered innocent) by faith in Christ, we can rightly say that our works don't gain us God's approval and favor. Christ, not works, makes us pleasing to God. If we think we are only partially pleasing to God, we will seek to gain approval from our works for God, from people, or from some other source. When we were saved by grace and justified, the Father put His full stamp of approval on us and said, "This is My Son [this refers to the privileges of "sonship" so it applies to both men and women] in whom I am well pleased." *In Christ, we are fully pleasing to Him right now!* God accepts Jesus, and because we are in Him, God accepts us. We don't have to constantly wonder if He is pleased with us; we can know it for certain. Try saying this: "In Christ, Father God is fully pleased with me. God is proud of me. God loves me." When we live in this reality, we are much more apt to "walk in a manner worthy of the Lord, fully pleasing Him." *In Christ, we live and operate from a place of acceptance and approval, not a place of rejection and striving.* The Father's view of us never changes. It's not based on our merit or good works; it's based in whether or not we have a relationship with His Son. He doesn't view us based upon our feelings (thank God), but rather through His redeeming work on the cross.

Fathers Discipline Their Children

When we go through difficult things or receive correction or discipline, some interpret that to mean God doesn't love us or care about us. In fact, it's quite the opposite. His Word instructs us, "those whom the Lord loves, He disciplines, and He scourges every son whom He receives" (Hebrews 12:6). Later on in the same chapter, it goes on to say:

> If you are without discipline, of which all have become partakers, then you are illegitimate children and not sons. Furthermore, we had earthly fathers to discipline us, and we respected them; shall we not much rather be subject to the Father of spirits, and live? For they disciplined us for a short time, as seemed best to them, but He disciplines us for our good, that we may share His holiness. All discipline for the moment seems not to be joyful, but sorrowful; yet to those who have been trained by it, afterwards, it yields the peaceful fruit of righteousness. (Hebrews 12:8-11 NASB)

When we go through difficult times, it's not always discipline; sometimes it's just life! If you wonder whether or not you are being disciplined for something, ask God, and He will tell you. He is not trying to hide it from you. If you don't hear from Him, assume it's something else. There are other reasons why hardships come: trials, disobedience, life, and so forth. It could be any one of a number of things. I am confident God will show you if you seek Him.

Wounds

In the beginning of this chapter, I shared a story about a father and son who went fishing together. Imagine if the son would have read his father's rendition of that day. He surely would have been deeply wounded. *Harsh words create wounds.* Harsh words from fathers have a way of cutting and wounding, and a lack of words can sometimes be even worse. Other abuses from fathers or father figures can deal blows that are hard to recover from—things like physical abuse, emotional abuse, lack of quality time spent together, refusal to be there when their children needed them, alcohol, drugs, divorce, addictions, poor treatment of women, rejection, humiliation, belittling—the list is long. *Fathers have the power to bless or to curse!* As the God-ordained leader of the family, their authority can bring great blessing or a curse.

In the movie, *Walk the Line* (about Johnny Cash), Johnny's father inflicted a crushing blow. When Johnny was a young boy, he and his older brother were sawing logs at a sawmill for money. Near the end, Johnny was getting antsy to go fishing, and his brother released him to go. Johnny was walking home when suddenly his dad and the family doctor came speeding up to him in their vehicle. When Johnny got home, he saw his brother lying on the bed, sliced open from stomach to chest, bleeding to death. He died later that day. After it happened, Johnny was at home listening to his radio, as was his custom. His dad came home in a drunken rampage and began to rail on him, *"It should have been you! God took the wrong one!"* Imagine the damage those words would cause a young boy.[3]

Words like this wound people in a way that's hard to recover from. They cut right to the very heart. They are like shackles from which you can't break free. But God wants to set this generation free from the wounds of fathers. These wounding words have been like a glass ceiling, causing you not to be able to rise above a certain point, but God is saying, "No more!" He wants to bring freedom and healing to this generation, to those who have been wounded and cut to the heart by their fathers.

This issue is key for you as you grow into adulthood. If you don't experience healing in this area, you will live out of your wounds instead of confidence in Christ. There are many ways this could play out. For women with father wounds, there may be a lack of real intimacy with your father. It's easy to long for intimacy with a man, and you may act this out in ways you never expected. In a cry for intimacy, Many women may give their bodies to men who simply show them attention. Some get into relationships with men who are like their dysfunctional fathers, rather than healthy, respectful men who will treat them well.

For men with father wounds: you may give yourself over to acting out in ways that try to cover and mask your hurt–addictive behaviors, poor treatment of women, and rebellion toward authority, for example. Maybe you feel abandoned by your father and you operate out of that orphan spirit by keeping healthy male relationships and mentorships at bay.

I'm not confining you to these things, but simply pointing out there may be issues in your life that need further exploration and healing.

The start to the journey of healing is forgiveness. We must start by forgiving our fathers. Many of them didn't know what they were doing (see Luke 23:34). Many of them just didn't have the "tools" or "equipment" to father us well. They were dealing with their own wounds and disabilities while trying to father us. Regardless of how hard it is, we must begin the process of forgiveness. Forgiveness is not a choice for followers of Christ; it is a command. God always gives us the grace to follow His commands. Unforgiveness is sin, and it will keep us bound in prison.

> Put on then, as God's chosen ones, holy and beloved, compassionate hearts, kindness, humility, meekness, and patience, bearing with one another and, if one has a complaint against another, forgiving each other; as

> the Lord has forgiven you, *so you also must forgive.*
> (Colossians 3:12-13, italics mine)

And again:

> For if you forgive others their trespasses, your heavenly
> Father will also forgive you, but if you do not forgive
> others their trespasses, neither will your Father forgive
> your trespasses. (Matthew 6:14-15)

In order to receive forgiveness, you must extend it. That is a kingdom principle. As you do this, God will release your heart to love. This most likely will not be a quick or easy process. You may actually find yourself having to do some repenting to your father. That was the case for me. I would encourage you to start by forgiving them out loud, like this:

Father, I forgive _____(insert your father's name) for _____ (name the ways he hurt you).

Something is released when you say it out loud. You may have to do it day after day, even about the same issues, as a step of faith. I would also encourage you to share with a mature and trusted brother or sister in the Lord, a spiritual parent, or a pastor or leader in your life. The healing process can be deeper, faster and more meaningful when you process with others. In your confession and transparency with others, you can find healing.

> Therefore, confess your sins to one another and pray
> for one another, that you may be healed. The prayer

> of a righteous person has great power as it is working.
> (James 5:16)

My friend says sin is like an open wound, and confession begins to close up the wound and forms a scab over it. Whether it's your sin or your father's sin, there is something to be said for sharing it with someone you trust.

Turning Back A Generation

A turning back to the Father heart of God is happening among our generation. As God promised in Malachi 4:5-6, He will send Elijah the prophet, who "will restore the hearts of the fathers to their children and the hearts of the children to their fathers."

In Elijah's day, there was a mass exodus of those leaving God to worship Baal (see 1 Kings 18 and 19). In judgment, the Lord caused it not to rain for three years and six months at the word of Elijah. After this time of drought (both physically and spiritually), the Lord told Elijah to show himself to the wicked king Ahab, and He would send rain on the earth. When he finally found Ahab, he asked him to bring all of Israel, as well as the 450 prophets of Baal and the 400 prophets of Asherah, up to the top of Mount Carmel for a showdown—God vs. Baal. How does this apply to us? *Baal* actually means "lord or possessor." In fact, at one time, the name was used for God, but eventually came to represent a totally different deity. Here are some of the things that were involved with Baal worship in Elijah's day: sexual perversion, homosexuality, violence, death, prostitution, divorce, covenant breaking, racial strife, unfaithfulness, self-mutilation, and cutting. Do any of these sound familiar? Maybe you are dealing with some of these things yourself.

The children of Israel were faltering between two opinions, and the prophet Elijah challenged them, "'If the LORD is God, follow him; but if Baal, then follow him,' but the people did not answer him a word" (1 Kings 18:21). They needed an awakening. They needed to see and experience God for themselves. As the story goes, they each (Elijah and the prophets of Baal) cut a bull into pieces, lay it on wood, and put no fire to it. They then called upon the name of their God, determining that "the God who answers by fire, he is God" (1 Kings 18:24). Elijah let the prophets of Baal go first. They called on Baal from morning until noon, but nothing happened. Elijah, being the gentle prophet that he was, began trash-talking:

> At noon, Elijah began making fun of them. "Pray louder!" he said. "Baal must be a god. Maybe he's day-dreaming or using the toilet or traveling somewhere. Or maybe he's asleep, and you have to wake him up." (1 Kings 18:27 CEV)

The false prophets began doing the thing you would expect. They yelled even louder and cut themselves with swords and knives until the blood was gushing. They did this until the time of the evening sacrifice, when everyone was bored and disinterested. Enter Elijah. He rebuildt the altar that had been torn down on top of Mount Carmel—the place used to worship God, which represented something significant that God had done in the past. Just for kicks, he dug a trench around the bull and poured four huge water pots over the sacrifice, filling the trench completely. Then he prayed this prayer:

> At the time of the offering of the evening sacrifice, Elijah the prophet came near and said, "O LORD, the God of Abraham, Isaac and Israel, today let it be known that You are God in Israel and that I am Your servant and I have done all these things at Your word. Answer me, O LORD, answer me, that this people may know

> that You, O LORD, are God, *and that You have turned their heart back again."* (1 Kings 18:36-37 NASB)

When God answered by fire, there was a turning back of a generation to Father God. In our time, God wants this generation, which has been captivated by Baal, to be captivated by Him, and He is willing to show His power in order that they may believe Him. For too long, we have been captivated by the things of this world. The Church is in desperate need of a revelation of the Father heart of God and His power. We are an experiential generation. We don't just want to hear about it; we want to see and experience it. As the story goes, "When all the people saw it, they fell on their faces and they said, 'the Lord, He is God, the Lord, He is God'" (1 Kings 18:39).

It's time for a *God versus Baal* showdown, and there is only one person who can win. The story ends with the prophets of Baal being slain, a torrential downpour of rain (Oh, how we need the Lord's rain!), and later the death of Ahab's evil wife, Jezebel. God showed Himself strong.

Do you ever wonder, why doesn't God show Himself strong like this anymore? I think we may be asking the wrong question. In the words of the late Leonard Ravenhill:

> To the question, "Where is the Lord God of Elijah?" We answer, "Where He has always been—on the throne!" But where are the Elijah's of God?[4]

God is powerful; there is no question about that. The real question is, when will we walk in the power of God? It has always been available, waiting for a people willing to forsake all to follow Him. The cry of my heart is to see a authentic move of God in our day, in our land, among our generation. I believe God wants to do it. How badly do you want it? Do you want it on your campus? Do you want it in your life? Do you want it among your generation? If you see it, I believe you can have it! Or are you too busy serving Baal to notice it?

Discussion Questions and Application

1. In what ways are you viewing God through the lens of your earthly father, either good or bad? In what ways do your views of God need to change in accordance with Scripture?
2. Identify the wounds that have been given to you by your father or "father-like" authority figures and begin the healing process by forgiving them.
3. Spend a quiet-reflective time with God allowing Him to speak over you through His Word and Spirit. Allow His Word to be the final say about your identity.
4. One of the primary ways father wounds can play out is in the spirit of abandonment. Many times, if we were abandoned either physically or emotionally, we live out of that hurt in our relationship to others, especially male authority figures. You don't have to search for it if it's not there, but allow God to speak to you about this and ask Him if you are living out of abandonment.
5. What is your real name? Who are you to God?

Meditation Verse

See what kind of love the Father has given to us, that we should be called children of God; and so we are. (1 John 3:1)

CHAPTER 6

IDENTITY PART 2: THE SPIRIT OF ADOPTION

Who are we in Christ? First and foremost, we are His sons and daughters. I don't know about you, but there are times when I struggle with my acceptance as one of God's children. There are times I struggle with condemnation and guilt when I blow it, equating my acceptance by God with my performance. I came from a broken home, dysfunctional and abusive, so sometimes I have a hard time identifying what "being a part of the family of God" and "being a son of God" looks like. At times I struggle with obedience, knowing God wants one thing, but instead I do another, failing again and again instead of being led by the Spirit of God.

Maybe you come from a broken home, a single-parent family, had two parents (maybe they were both the same sex), but one or both was abusive. Maybe you have one step-parent or two, maybe you have no siblings, or maybe you have several. Maybe you were the favorite child, or maybe you were the black sheep. Maybe your relationship with your parents is fantastic, or maybe it's dysfunctional and limping along or even non-existent. Maybe you feel part of a family, or maybe you don't! Wherever you are in this natural life doesn't represent where you are in God's eyes!

The Scripture tells us *we have received the Spirit of adoption that leads us away from sin and toward the Father and confirms us as children of God and heirs of Christ!*

> For all who are being led by the Spirit of God, these are sons of God. For you have not received a spirit of slavery leading to fear again, but you have received a spirit of adoption as sons by which we cry out, "Abba! Father!" The Spirit Himself testifies with our spirit that we are children of God, and if children, heirs also, heirs of God and fellow heirs with Christ, if indeed we suffer with Him so that we may also be glorified with Him. (Romans 8:14-17 NASB)

Romans 8:15 tells us that we can identify sons and daughters of God by whether or not they are *being led (continual, present tense) by the Spirit of God!* This does not mean we don't have failures, but that we are constantly in the process of being led (which implies we follow) by the Spirit of God. To be *led* means to bring, drive, go, or induce.[1] Bible commentator Albert Barnes describes it as a willingness to yield to His influence and submit to Him.

The Holy Spirit doesn't just hand us a map; He is our guide. There is a big difference between having a map and having a guide. Picture the Bible as the map and the Holy Spirit as the interpreter. In a way, the Holy Spirit guides us like a GPS unit. He is leading us where we need to go and giving us turn-by-turn instructions. But we need to hear what He is saying *and* be willing to follow Him wherever He leads. He will direct us again and again, but in the end, it is our choice either to follow Him or not. It's not that He won't give us second chances, but sometimes we miss the divine opportunity that He was leading us toward.

Jesus is our great example. In Matthew 4, Jesus was *led* or *driven* into the wilderness *by the Spirit.* Sometimes we go to the wilderness because of disobedience, and sometimes we are led there by our obedience. In this case, it was because of His obedience that Jesus was led into the wilderness. Here's my point: Jesus was led by the Spirit of God in a constant way, sometimes to places that weren't pleasant—*like the wilderness and the cross!*

There are countless examples in the New Testament of Jesus being led by the Spirit of God, thus proving that He was the Son of God.

So, where are we being led? There are specific places and things that the Holy Spirit will lead us into, but in general, we are being led away from sin and towards the Father. Romans 8:13 tells us, "If by the Spirit we put to death the deeds of the body, we will live." The deeds of the body are those driven by our fleshly, selfish, and sinful desires. Jesus tells us that if we love Him we will keep His commandments, and then later He says that we are His friends if we do whatever He commands (see John 14:15 and 15:14). It may sound controlling, but it's really not. His heart is to protect us and keep us on the right path. He helps us to turn away from sin and toward the Father. Remember, *true sons and daughters of God are led by the Spirit, away from sin and towards the Father!*

When we are adopted into the family of God, He gives us the name, place, privilege, and authority of a fully matured son or daughter. This is profound. Scripture tells us we have not received the spirit of slavery, which leads us to fear again, but we have received the spirit of adoption as children, which leads us to we cry out, "Abba Father" (see Romans 8:15). Adoption in that day and age was defined as, "The giving to any one the *name* and *place* and *privileges* of a son who is not a son by birth."[2] In essence, we receive all the same privileges without being natural-born children!

When you were born again, you came into the family of God and received the family name. That's very important. In fact, without that, you can't even see the kingdom of God (see John 3:3), but it's only the first step! It's this idea of *place* (referring to your position) and *privileges* that I want to talk more about. The idea being established here is that adopted sons and daughters have just as much right and privilege as natural sons and daughters! So, being adopted isn't simply about coming into the family; it's about inheriting all that belongs to Christ. Listen to what author Dutch Sheets says about this:

> The word translated "adoption" (*huiothesia*, literally "the placing of a son") is not referring to a child being placed (*thesia*) into a family but rather a child already in the family being placed into the authority of a fully matured son (*huios*). It's about jurisdiction and rights, not entering the family.[3]

Picture it like a bar mitzvah of sorts. A bar mitzvah happens when a Jewish young man becomes fully responsible (at age thirteen) to observe the commands of the Torah. It's a "coming of age" ceremony. In a similar way, the spirit of adoption is a coming of age concerning who you are, your authority in Christ, and the taking up of your place in the family as a fully matured son or daughter!

In Greek and Roman society during this day, a boy being adopted ceased to belong to his own family and was, in every respect, bound to the person who had adopted him, as if he were his own child, and at the death of his adopting father, he possessed his estates. If a person, after he had adopted a child, happened to have children of his own, then the estate was equally divided between the adopted and real children.[4] This is amazing! It would be easy to think of adopted children as "second rate" or not on the same playing field as natural children, but it's exactly the opposite in God's kingdom. Adopted children have every right and privilege as natural children, and God loves them just as much!

A friend of mine tells it this way. What if Prince William of Wales had amnesia and you saw him digging around in a garbage can right in your town or city? What would you say to him? You would probably say something like, "What are you, of all people, doing digging around in a garbage can? Don't you know who you are?" You would think he is crazy. After all, he is the son of a king. He probably carries more cash in his pocket than you get paid in a month! Ironically, many of us do the same thing. We are like princes and princesses with amnesia. We dig around in garbage cans looking for scraps when we are sons and daughters of royalty. We only do this because we don't know who we are!

A huge part of Romans 8:15 deals with how the spirit of adoption allows us to cry out, "Abba Father." *When we receive the spirit of adoption, we are led away from sin and toward the Father. He then gives us the name, place, privilege, and authority of a fully matured son or daughter!*

> But to as many as did receive and welcome Him, He gave the authority (power, privilege, right) to become the children of God, that is, to those who believe in (adhere to, trust in, and rely on) His name. (John 1:12 AMP)

Did you catch that? He has given us *authority* to become children of God and heirs with Jesus Christ (with God Himself)! Because of our family name (which signifies our place, privilege, and authority), we are heirs of everything Christ has. Jesus is our greatest reward, but we also inherit everything that goes with Him. I once heard Jack Hayford say,

> The only reason we (the sons and daughters in my family) got an inheritance from my mother was not because we were worthy, but because we carry the name "Hayford." We automatically received the inheritance because of our name.

Jesus carries the name "I AM," and we carry the name "His." Look at Romans 8:17: "...and if children, heirs also, heirs of God and fellow heirs with Christ, if indeed we *suffer* with Him so that we may also be glorified". The root word for suffer is *passion.* Sometimes families experience suffering. It's a normal part of life. As family, we are in it for the long haul until one day there will be no more suffering. What kind of family would we be if the minute we experience suffering we abandon the rest of the family? It's the suffering that qualifies us to be glorified with Him. *If we are not willing to suffer with Him, we are not qualified to be glorified.*

I like to say it this way: *That which we are passionate about we are willing to suffer for.* It's not that Jesus wants to hurt us; nothing could be further from the truth. Jesus certainly never promised that life with Him would be problem-free; in fact, in many ways, life becomes harder when we come to Jesus (see John 16:33). We have a real enemy who is bent on making us fall. When we live out our kingdom purpose, we are wreaking havoc on the kingdom of darkness. On the other hand, there is nothing as fulfilling as knowing Christ, finding who we are in Him, and living out His purpose for our lives. We can't put a price tag on waking up every day with a sense of belonging and purpose. My point is, as the body of Christ, we are family, and families go through hardship together. We don't abandon our family simply because things get tough; instead, we pull closer together!

Suffering Brings Maturation

Gina and I went through a hellish year in 2007. It was as if God was testing and shaking everything in our lives. Now that I look back, I believe He was preparing us for what was to come – church planting in one of the most difficult and least churched areas of the country–Boston! Our finances were severely tested (almost causing us to leave the ministry), our marriage was the rockiest it had ever been, and the level of personal temptation we experienced was at an all-time high. It was a difficult and painful year. There were times I wanted to cash everything in and walk away. It literally lasted all of 2007 and a few months into 2008. In the midst of it, we knew God was preparing us to "give birth" to something. We were carrying a vision inside of our hearts, and we knew it was time for it to come forth. In the process, He was speaking to us about "acceleration." I am much more cautious now when I hear that word from God or I hear other people telling me that God is bringing "acceleration." Webster's Dictionary defines acceleration as, "to cause faster development, progress, or advancement." At the time He spoke it, I immediately thought of more preaching engagements, greater opportunities, and larger impact, but I've now come to understand it in a different way. God's thoughts and ways are not our thoughts and ways (see Isaiah 55:8-9).

In Psalm 103, the Psalmist says that the children of Israel knew the acts of God, but that Moses knew the *ways* of God. There is a big difference. We can know the acts of God from a distance, but His ways can only be learned up close. When God speaks a word to us, many times it has much more meaning than we attach to it. We think one way, and God thinks another.

I was looking for outward signs of acceleration but God was accelerating our inner growth—and that was painful! It's like hitting a massive growth spurt during your adolescent years. Those who grow several inches in one year usually experience some side effects—pain in their joints and limbs, as well as clumsiness, weakness, and coordination problems. Spiritual growth and acceleration is not much different! We are clumsy, off balance, and weak. We experience pain and discomfort as growth comes at an accelerated rate.

God is interested in our character before our calling. I have prayed this prayer regularly throughout the years and God has honored it: "God, don't allow me to get to a place where my character can't keep me!"

I want to encourage and caution you. Acceleration in His kingdom is awesome, but it also means accelerated growth on the inside. So be ready, keep your focus on Jesus, and let Him have His way. He will sustain you through every growing pain, all your clumsiness, and all your weakness to get the end result: Christ in you, the hope of glory (see Col. 1:27).

A Final Word

God is always working to conform us to the image of Christ. We have the unique privilege of being His sons and daughters in His kingdom with an inheritance. *As sons and daughters of God, we have received the spirit of adoption, who leads us away from sin and toward the Father. He gives us the name, place, privilege, and authority of a fully matured son or daughter.*

Discussion Questions

1. If you have never come into the family of God by receiving the gift of salvation, that's the first step. If you have not done this and would like to, please ask one of the people in your small group study to lead you in a prayer of repentance and salvation, making Jesus Christ your Savior, Lord, and Master!
2. Would you say you are "led" by the Spirit of God as it says in Romans 8:14? Remember, it means being driven or possessing a willingness to yield to His influence and submit to Him. Are you consistently obeying the Spirit's leading toward the Father and away from sin?
3. Have you recognized your place in Christ—your name, place, and privileges that have been given to you as a son or daughter of God? Have you been acting like a prince or princess digging in a garbage can, unaware of who you are?
4. Study and say out loud the list of confessions for one week (these can be found in Appendix B).
5. Over the next week, please write out and spend time meditating on this statement: *As sons and daughters of God, we have received the Spirit of Adoption who leads us away from sin and toward the Father. He gives us the name, place, privilege, and authority of a fully matured son or daughter.*

Imagine what it might be like if you lived like you belong to God as His fully matured child?

Resources

Appendix B: "Who Am I in Christ" by Kent A. Murawski

Meditation Verse

> Because you are sons, God sent the Spirit of his Son into our hearts, the Spirit who calls out, "Abba, Father." (Galatians 4:6 NIV)

CHAPTER 7

IDENTITY PART 3: KNOW THYSELF

Knowing Him

Sometimes we think we know ourselves, only to find out we can't figure ourselves out. Why do we do the things we do? Why do we think the way we think? Why do we feel the way we feel? Then there are larger questions like: Why am I here? Where did I come from? What on earth am I supposed to be doing? But there is something infinitely more important than knowing yourself. The answers to those questions are all found in *knowing Him.* The reality is you can't know yourself until you know Him. The chief aim of our lives is to know Him. Out of that, everything else comes.

Whenever you see a defining work of art, a masterpiece, for example, it begs the question: *Who is the artist?* If shown a picture of *Starry Night,* virtually everyone knows who the artist is. In fact, I don't know of a masterpiece with an unknown artist. Maybe there is one, but if so, it's rare. Just as with a piece of art, it's impossible to look at God's masterpiece, the human being, and not see design and intentionality. *Our identity is undeniably linked to the One who created us.* You wouldn't look at the Michelangelo's *Mona Lisa,* listen to Mozart's *Symphony No. 40 in G minor*, or watch Shakespeare's *Romeo and Juliet* without wondering who the artist is. Why? Because *creation is defined by its creator.* Just as those classic works had a creator, we were designed by the Great Artist and were meant to point to Him.

In the famous passage about the Church (see Matthew 16:13-

19), Jesus asks His disciples a direct question: "Who do people say that the Son of Man is? They answer honestly and say, "Some say John the Baptist, some Elijah, and others Jeremiah or one of the prophets." The Scripture doesn't say this, but I think Jesus looked right into their eyes with His soul piercing gaze and says, "But who do *you* say that I am?" (Matthew 16:15, italics mine) His question goes from general to specific. Suddenly there is quiet. You could hear a pin drop. That's a question that penetrates the soul. And He is asking each of us that very same question right now: _____ (insert your name), who do *you* say that I am?

The disciples had probably learned by then, after watching Jesus interact with the Pharisees and being around Him for a time, that He didn't ask questions like this because He wanted to know the answer. He asked questions to make a point or teach a lesson.

At some point, we must all grapple with this question. What was Jesus trying to say? Peter was the first one to answer, and oddly enough he got it right! He replied, "You are the Christ, the Son of the living God" (Matthew 16:16). Jesus replied, "Blessed are you, Simon Bar-Jonah! For flesh and blood has not revealed this to you, but My Father who is in heaven" (Matthew 16). After Peter had a revelation from the Father about who Jesus was, Jesus began to speak definition and destiny over Peter by saying, "*You are Peter*, and on this rock I will build my church, and the gates of hell shall not prevail against it" (Matthew 16, emphasis added). Here's the lesson:

In order to know who we are, we must first know who He is!

Our identity is found *in Christ*. Jesus told Peter that he learned this via revelation from the Father, and *revelation comes through relationship with the Son of God*. The whole Kingdom is founded on relationship. Think about how Jesus taught us to pray. The first words He taught us were, *"Our Father"* (Matthew 6:9). The Father wants to have relationship with us, and He provided a way for us to come to Him through the blood of Jesus! Jesus said, "Whoever has seen Me has seen the Father" (Matthew 14:9). Because Father God revealed it, Peter had perceived or clearly discerned Jesus' true identity. The word *revelation* means to "take off the cover, to disclose, or to reveal."[1] In essence, Jesus was saying, "You got it Peter! And because you've had a revelation of Me from My Father, now I am going to tell you who you are. *You are Peter* (meaning "rock") and on this rock I will build My Church.

Our chief aim is to know Him. Like Paul, we should count everything rubbish in order that we may gain Christ (see Phil. 3:8). Our desire should be to know nothing except Jesus Christ and Him crucified (see 1 Cor. 2:2).

Jesus provided the way for us to have access to the Father, but we still have to take the time to develop our relationship with God. A living, active, two-way relationship with God really is the most important thing–surpassing all else. When I stand before Jesus, this is *not* what I want to hear Him say:

> On that day many will say to me, "Lord, Lord, did we not prophesy in your name, and cast out demons in your name, and do many mighty works in your name?" And then will I declare to them, "I never knew you; depart from me, you workers of lawlessness." (Matthew 7:22-23 ESV)

Who is He to you? Is He Jesus, the Christ, the Son of the Living God? Is He Savior, Redeemer, Anointed One, and Messiah? Have you put your trust in Him? Do you know Him? Is He God's only begotten Son, seated at the right hand of the Father, the Lord of everything, including your life? Does He have the ultimate say in what you do, who you marry, and where you go, what job you work? Do you believe that Jesus came as a baby, lived a perfect life, died as the perfect sacrifice to stand in your place and take the punishment you deserved? Did He rise again from the dead in order to set you free from sin and establish His kingdom? Do you have an ongoing, life-giving, intimate love relationship with the Father, Son, and Holy Spirit? Remember, revelation of Jesus comes through relationship. *You can't know who you are if you don't know Him!*

Know Thyself

As I have already mentioned, we can't possibly know who we are until we know who He is. Once we begin to know who He is (and this is a life long endeavor) then we can begin to know who we are and what we have in Christ. It's a growing and consistent revelation that everything Jesus is and has belongs to us. We are joint heirs with Christ (see Romans 8:17).

There is a scene in *The Matrix* (part 1 of the trilogy) where Neo, the main character, goes to see a prophetess in the world of the Matrix. The Matrix is a dream world created by a massive computer program, into which most everyone on earth is hardwired, thereby allowing the machines to keep people under control and use them as an energy source. Essentially, the machines have reduced people to batteries. But there are some "freedom fighters" who have been freed from the Matrix. These freedom fighters live their lives hiding from the machines and hacking their way into the Matrix in order to free others and defeat the machines. Rather than being controlled by the Matrix, they can now go back into the Matrix fully awake and aware. Neo has been told by Morpheus, the leader of the resistance, that he is "the One." An almost a savior-like character, Neo would be able to do whatever he wants within the virtual world of the Matrix, thus defeating the machines forever. As Neo walks into the kitchen of the prophetess, it is a surreal scene from the 1970s. She is a motherly-looking woman smoking a cigarette while finishing a batch of cookies. After observing him for a few minutes, she points to a sign above the door. The sign happens to be in Latin. It says, "Temet Nosce," which in Latin means, "Know Thyself." In Greek it's, "Nosce te ipsum" and means the same thing. Although used throughout history as a calling card to exalt "Self," the profound-yet-hidden truth of it lies in this: *One can not know thyself without knowledge of the Creator, Jesus Christ.*

Neo did not know who he was. The prophetess looks at his hands for a moment and asks, "Are you the One?" Neo pauses for a few moments and says, "I'm not the One." She goes on, "Being the One is like being in love. No one can tell you; you just know it. You have the gift, but it looks like you are waiting for something." "What?" Neo asks. The prophetess retorts, "I don't know, maybe another life." This whole freedom thing was new to Neo. He had spent the previous thirty years hardwired against his will into a virtual world. He had been a slave, so he had a hard time knowing who he was in this new context, let alone believing he was really the One.

Now, we are certainly not "the One"; that title belongs to Jesus alone. But like Neo, we have powers yet to be discovered, authority we never dreamed of, and the favor of an all-powerful God. I see many followers of Jesus like Neo, walking around confused and scared, not knowing who they are and thinking they have to wait for heaven or another season. They have been "hard-wired" into the world's system of thinking, when in actuality *they are sons and daughters of the Most High God and the King of Kings.* We often say, "King of Kings" without even realizing what we are saying. That means He is the King over all other worldly kings and kingdoms. We have been adopted and given the full rights, privileges, and authority of natural children (see Romans 8:15).

God even defines us as "kings and priests" (see Revelation 1:6). Remember, we have His DNA and are in His bloodline. The first two chapters of Ephesians tell us that we are far above principalities and powers and might and dominion because we are seated with Him in heavenly places *in Christ!* We have been given the keys (authority) of the kingdom and the authority to bind and loose, or forbid and permit (see Matt. 16:19). This progressive realization of who we are and our authority in Christ will rise until we one day rule and reign with God when "The kingdom of the world has become the kingdom of our Lord and of His Christ; and He will reign forever and ever" (see Revelation 11:15).

Identity

Identity is one of the most important issues, not only in young adulthood, but throughout life. Unlike in other religions, our identity is established in the identity of someone else. We have heard the statement, "It's hard to know where you're going if you don't know where you've been." For our purposes, I would like to alter it to this: "It's hard to know who you are unless you know *who* you came from." Our identity is wrapped up in Jesus and what He has done on our behalf. The moment we are born again, we become new creations in Christ, and the DNA of Jesus is planted deep within us. As believers, we are transformed into His image and we begin to "find" ourselves as we behold Him and see Him face-to-face (see 2 Corinthians 3:18).

As we discussed earlier, we have been justified or rendered innocent. Unlike Hinduism and reincarnation where people strive to become better with each passing life until they "arrive," in Christianity, the moment we are born again, we are rendered innocent of all our past sins by the blood of Jesus. His blood is what matters, not our works. It is all based on Him. We are righteous only because He shed His perfect blood on the cross. What this means in plain English is *God will never love us more or less than He does at the moment of our salvation because His love is not dependent on what we do; it's dependent on what He has already done.* I have heard it said, "There are no good people in heaven, only forgiven ones." This is the difference between justification and works. A works mentality causes us to constantly strive with the false reality that we are not good enough and need to keep doing better so God will love us. *In Christ* means we are already accepted and we operate out of a place of love and acceptance rather than a place of inadequacy and striving.

Entering this place of love and acceptance comes by revelation (taking off the veil). I operated in a works mentality for many years and still find myself doing so from time to time. It was an awful place to live—thinking I constantly had to do more and perform better for God to love me and accept me. I lived with a sense of guilt and condemnation every time I messed up. Many of you know what I'm talking about, and many of you are there right now. Why didn't someone teach me this the instant I was saved? It would have saved me a lot of heartache! Many times, God will allow us to stay in "works" mentality until we realize that we can't do it! We can't defeat sin on our own. We can't be good people on our own. We can't do Christianity on our own. We are wholly dependent upon Him to be holy.

So who are you?

Discussion Questions

1. What is more important than knowing yourself? Why?
2. Picture Jesus standing in front of you asking you the same question He asked Peter: "Who do you say that I am?" What would your answer be? Do you believe it?
3. If your answer to that question is, "I don't know?" What are you going to do about it?

Meditation Verse

He said to them, "But who do you say that I am?" (16) Simon Peter replied, "You are the Christ, the Son of the living God." (Matthew 16:15-16)

PART 4

RIGHT RELATIONSHIPS

Relationships are of the utmost importance. Gary Smalley says, "Life is relationships. The rest are just details." This section is all about the crucial relationships in your life. You will learn how to navigate the important relationships during your college years, including: your relationship with the body of Christ (you are one small part, interconnected with other parts), your relationships with the opposite sex as a single adult, and relationships with friends who will compliment your walk with God and position you for maximum growth!

CHAPTER 8

ROOTED AND PLANTED

You've probably heard the expression that God is all you need and that He is your everything. Though there is truth to this, it doesn't quite tell the whole story. God has designed us to need other people as well. The bottom line is this: *It's impossible to thrive spiritually on your own.* One of the most important steps to thriving in your faith is to become planted in a local church. For the record, I don't care if it's a big church, small church, house church, or something in between. The terminology or style is not important, but connecting yourself to a body of believers where Jesus calls you to be planted is absolutely vital.

So many young people struggle to fit church in among their many commitments. College sports, extracurricular activities, jobs, and leisure all fight for a place, but if you want to thrive spiritually, *the local church must become one of the major building blocks in your life.* I'm not saying you need to be doing a Christian activity every night of the week, but I am saying you need a vital connection to other believers in a local church. I often see students giving preference to sports, their studies, or extracurricular activities. Over time, they fade out of the local church–often to the demise of their walk with God. In our day and age, if you let the powers that be know of your religious convictions, there should be no problem in missing a practice or activity for a Sunday service or a small group. It's simply a matter of priority. Look at it this way–if a Muslim needed to get out of something for a religious purpose, don't think for a second that the coach, leader, or group would even raise an eyebrow. Even in our jobs, I have never had any trouble whatsoever in letting my employer know I can't work Sunday mornings and/ or a specific week night because of a faith commitment. *Your life should revolve around God's will, not sports, academics, or extracurricular activities.* Part of God's will for you is gathering together with other believers for mutual strength, growth, and encouragement.

> We should keep on encouraging each other to be thoughtful and to do helpful things. Some people have gotten out of the habit of meeting for worship, but we must not do that. We should keep on encouraging each other, especially since you know that the day of the Lord's coming is getting closer. (Hebrews 10:24-25 CEV)

The Church Is Not a Building

Church refers to people, not a building. It is a company of believers, not an institution or organization.[1] In our culture and day, we have minimized the term *church* to mean a building, when in reality, people are the temple of the Holy Spirit (see 1 Corinthians 6:19). The Greek word for church is *ekklesia*. It also means "those called out" and often refers to "an assembly or congregation."[2] The word *ekklesia* has deeper roots than even the New Testament. Throughout the Greek world, leading up to New Testament times (see Acts 19:39), *ekklesia* was the:

> Designation of the regular assembly of the whole body of citizens in a free city-state, "called out" by the herald for the discussion and decision of public business. To the Greek it meant a self-governing democratic society; but to the Jew, *a theocratic society whose members were the subjects of the Heavenly King* (italics mine).[3]

Although it shares the same roots as the Greek meaning, the Christian meaning has an important nuance, referring more to a "theocratic democracy"—a free society always aware that their freedom is derived from obedience to a heavenly King.[4] We belong to Him and are part of a greater assembly that has been called out of darkness and into His glorious light!

A Part, Not the Whole

In building terms, we are each *one* stone, but it takes *many* stones to make up a building. When we don't allow God to plant us in a local expression of His Church to experience Christian community, not only are we handicapped, but the rest of the body is deficient without us!

> And now you are living stones that are being used to build a spiritual house. You are also a group of holy priests, and with the help of Jesus Christ you will offer sacrifices that please God. (1 Peter 2:5 CEV)

It's impossible to be the Church by yourself because the very essence of the word points to a "Christian community." That rules out Internet or television as the only form of practicing your faith. It can be a good supplement, but not the primary expression of your faith.

> Now the body is not made up of *one* part but of *many*. If the foot should say, "Because I am not a hand, I do not belong to the body," it would not for that reason cease to be part of the body. And if the ear should say, "Because I am not an eye, I do not belong to the body," it would not for that reason cease to be part of the body. If the whole body were an eye, where would the sense of hearing be?

> If the whole body were an ear, where would the sense of smell be? But in fact God has arranged the parts in the body, every one of them, just as he wanted them to be. (1 Corinthians 12:14-18 NIV)

Simply said, *we need one another.* We are deficient without each other. God never planned us to live life alone. Right from the very beginning, God said, "It is not good for man to be alone" (Genesis 2:18). You are selling yourself, others, and God short when you aren't deeply rooted in a Christian community.

Fellowship Redefined

Christian community is not to be taken lightly. If the Church is made up of people, then part of being rooted and planted is being in deeply committed relationships with other people who make up the Church! The word *community* comes from the Greek word for fellowship, *koinonia.* When people say the word *fellowship,* depending on our background, we may think of a pot-luck dinner in the "fellowship" hall or people casually talking together over cookies, donuts, or finger foods. This couldn't be further from the truth. Let's look deeper into this word, *koinonia.* The word means partnership or participation, and carries with it the idea of communion together.

> koinōnia (koy-nohn-ee'-ah): *partnership,* that is, (literally) *participation,* or (social) *intercourse,* or (pecuniary) *benefaction:* - (to) communicate (-action), communion, (contri-), distribution, fellowship.[5]

Sometimes to understand what something is, we first need to understand what it is *not.* The following definitions of what fellowship is and is not, have been adapted from the book, *Why Small Groups* by C.J. Mahaney:[6]

Fellowship is *Not*:

1. *Warm human interchange (sharing common interests, experiences, or viewpoints) is not synonymous with fellowship.* For example, I like backpacking. Say I find someone else who likes backpacking and we have a twenty-minute conversation based on our interest and love for backpacking. Although stimulating, this is not what the word *koinonia* is referring to. Please don't misunderstand me, casual interchange, sharing common interests, or just hanging out is not bad, and in fact can be springboards or gateways into real fellowship. But in and of itself, sharing common interests does not represent true fellowship.
2. *Just because you attend a Bible study, men's rally, or church function does not mean you have experienced true biblical fellowship.* This is the same idea. You may go to a spiritual event, but not actually go any deeper than casual conversation with someone.

Let's start by giving an accurate definition of what *fellowship is:*

"Fellowship is participating together in the life and truth made possible by the Holy Spirit through our union with Christ. Fellowship is sharing something in common on the deepest possible level of human relationship—*our experience of God Himself".*[7]

When we look at fellowship this way, some of us may realize we are not really having it. This could be the reason we are so dissatisfied with our Christian walk. We were meant to experience deep communion and real relationship with others, and without it, we feel empty and dissatisfied. Fellowship is not a program or an event. It's not simply having coffee and cookies after a church service. *Fellowship is a way of life.* Fellowship is more accurately described as "the brotherhood."[8] It is an "I'll die for you and you die for me" type of relationship. Jesus said it this way: "Greater love has no one than this, to lay down His life for His friends" (John 15:13). Biblical fellowship involves the type of bond expressed by the Marine slogan, "No man left behind." We are in a war, caught between two worlds. We certainly don't just send in one man by himself to win the war. We are not Rambo or Arnold Schwarzenegger. No matter how many movies we have watched (or acted out in the mirror), we can't walk by faith or defeat the spiritual forces of darkness by ourselves.

There is a poignant clip in the *The Lord of the Rings: The Return of the King* that I think accurately portrays what true fellowship is like. Frodo and Sam have been making their way to Mordor to destroy the enemy's ring of power by throwing it into the very fires of Mount Doom where it was forged. Near the end, as Frodo and Sam are trudging up the volcano, Frodo can go no further. Sam urgently exhorts Frodo to keep going and says, "I can't carry the ring for you, Mr. Frodo, but I can carry you!" He hoists Frodo over his shoulder and, in agonizing pain, begins to stagger up the mountainside. The scene then cuts to the others, who make up the "Fellowship of the Ring" (those who came with Frodo on this journey to help him and protect him). They have come to the gates of Mordor and what they believe is certain death so they can draw away the gaze of the dark lord Sauron from Frodo and Sam. They are willing to sacrifice their lives so Frodo can succeed with the mission. As they face the hordes of Sauron, King Aragorn looks back at the others and says, "For Frodo!" Without considering themselves, they charge fiercely at the enemy army. This is a perfect picture of true fellowship.[9]

I often run into people who love God, but are not satisfied with their experience of Christ as it relates to their current experience of "church." They are longing for something more than just "going to church." Yes, it is absolutely biblical and necessary to assemble together for times of corporate worship and teaching, but it certainly should not be the only way we experience Jesus. I believe what we are missing is an experience with Jesus alongside others who are on mission together.

So I am advocating that you be part of a community of believers, a church, who are practicing their faith and engaging in *fellowship* in the true sense of the word. Find your band of brothers and sisters and follow Jesus together!

Rooted and Planted

> The righteous man will flourish like the palm tree, He will grow like a cedar in Lebanon. Planted in the house of the LORD, They will flourish in the courts of our God. (Psalm 92:12-13 NASB)

This passage is not necessarily about being planted in a physical house, but in a family or home. When we are planted in the house of the Lord, we are planted in a family of people. In this context, we will flourish in the courts of God. God has always been about family; in fact, He created it! *Family has always been the number-one context through which spiritual growth occurs.* He plants us in a spiritual family that we can call home, and in this loving and nurturing environment, where we can receive encouragement, care, correction, and rebuke, we begin to flourish and produce fruit!

I came to follow Christ my junior year of college. As I mentioned, my journey began at a conference for college students called Jubilee. After that, I had a desire to read my Bible, pray, and be in relationship with other believers, but I can't say I was living my life in Christian community. For one, I don't think most of the Christians in my campus fellowship really wanted to hang out with me too much because I probably scared them. No one had really discipled me, so I was trying to figure it all out on my own. In short, I was a mess.

It wasn't until I graduated from college and was planted in a family of believers in a local church that I really began to grow and flourish. As much as we want to say that any group of believers gathering together for fellowship constitutes a church, those gatherings don't always accomplish what the church is supposed to accomplish. So what is the church? For the most part, I really like Mark Driscoll's definition (and quite honestly haven't found many others):

> The local church is a community of regenerated believers who confess Jesus Christ as Lord. In obedience to Scripture they organize under qualified leadership, gather regularly for preaching and worship, observe the biblical sacraments of baptism and communion, are unified by the Spirit, are disciplined for holiness, scattered to fulfill the Great Commission and the Great Commandment, as missionaries to the world for God's glory and their joy.[10]

I think Driscoll makes some great points in this definition. To highlight and recap the necessary ingredients (with a couple additions of my own), here is what makes up a local church:

- Possessing qualified and called leadership;
- Gathering regularly for preaching and worship;
- Experiencing biblical fellowship on a regular basis;
- Observing biblical sacraments of baptism and communion;
- Unified by the Spirit;
- Disciplined for holiness (sanctification);
- Scattered to fulfill the Great Commission (see Matt. 28:18-20) and the Great Commandment (see Mark 12:30-31);
- Being sent as missionaries to the world for God's glory and our joy.

A short time after being rooted and planted in a church, God set me free from my addiction to pornography and the deception that I was homosexual. I also began to develop committed relationships and began to serve in youth ministry. I was flourishing in the courts of God. I grew steadily and quickly because I was planted in the house of God. A plant would struggle to keep growing if it was continually pulled up by the roots and put in different soil each week. But planted in the right soil and climate, watered and given plenty of light, and left to grow; it will flourish! At that time, I became aware of Psalm 92, and it has become a foundation in my life.

If you want to flourish in your walk with God, being planted in a church is an absolute necessity. As you leave home and your family of believers for college or a new job, it may take some time to develop deep, committed relationships and find a new family of believers. *I suggest you seek to maintain a solid connection with some people from your home church, especially until you find a new one.* If your church doesn't already have something set up to help you with this transition, it could be as simple as asking some people who will challenge you and keep in touch with you on a weekly basis (or even come visit you if necessary) until you find a committed family of believers.

Don't let the wave of spiritual resources through the Internet and television replace God's plan for you to become planted in His house and be a part of a spiritual family. *It's impossible to thrive in your faith if you live in willing isolation.* God desires believers to be rooted and planted so that they may grow into a flourishing tree in His house. Remember, you are but *one stone* in the spiritual house God is building.

Discussion Questions

1. Are you in committed relationship with a group of other believers with whom you are growing and changing? If so, how has it benefitted you? If not, why not?
2. Are you fulfilled in your life as a follower of Christ?
3. Did you learn anything new about what real biblical fellowship is? Please explain.
4. Are you having real biblical fellowship? If not, what can you do to find it or even develop it with other believers?

Recommended Resources

Believerscollegeprep.com – From securing the faith to reducing the cost of college, Believers College Prep is a centralized place for all things transition.
Why Small Groups by C.J. Mahaney

Meditation Verse

The righteous man will flourish like the palm tree, He will grow like a cedar in Lebanon. Planted in the house of the LORD, They will flourish in the courts of our God. (Psalm 92:12-13 NASB)

CHAPTER 9

OVERCOMING SEXUAL TEMPTATION

If you are going to thrive spiritually in the transition from high school to college and young adulthood, victory over sexual temptation is imperative. In this day and age, we face sexual temptation at every turn—through print, television, and the Internet. It's not possible to avoid it altogether. You must learn how to overcome this snare in order to have a successful walk with God, a successful life, successful relationships, and a healthy marriage. Sexual impurity has the potential to destroy your life. It can jeopardize your relationship with God, your marriage and family, and your finances. It is an offense against God and against your own body (see 1 Corinthians 6:18-20). Lust is not the unpardonable sin, but it is a very damaging one.

Here are some of the effects pornography and sexual immorality can have on your life:

- Pornography and lust create unrealistic and false expectations of what your spouse looks like or how he or she "performs" sexually. It introduces the betrayal and pain of adultery (whether physical or virtual, Jesus didn't differentiate between the two). It puts unrealistic pressure upon your wife to be like or perform like those whom you have watched or fantasized about. It is in every sense of the word, *adultery.*
- Pornography creates a fantasy world where you are in charge. You can access it any time you want and make anyone do anything you want. The problem is that *it's not real!*

- Sexual addiction, like any addiction, is very difficult to break. It can rule your life and cause immense pain as well as relational and financial ruin.
- Your sexuality, if not under the control of the Holy Spirit, has the potential to totally shipwreck your life and even bar you from entering heaven (see Gal. 5:19-21).

I was introduced to pornography at twelve years of age. Before the Internet, the average age that young people were exposed to pornography was between 11-13 years old. With the Internet, it can be as early as eight or nine years old,[1] and the largest users of pornography are those in the 12-17 age range.[2] My first exposure happened when a friend brought a pornographic magazine to a campout. We gazed at it for hours, fantasizing about what it would be like have sex with the pictured women. Something awakened in me that day that started an avalanche. I had no idea of the floodgate I had opened up. The enemy often snares us by opening up a "breach in the wall" at a young age. After my first exposure, I continued to engage in porn. By the age of sixteen, I was sexually active. In today's culture, sexual activity is beginning even earlier. There are stories of fifth graders having oral sex. According to the Centers for Disease Control and Prevention, more than half of 15-19 year olds are having oral sex and the report says, "It needn't even occur within the confines of a relationship."[3]

By the time I reached college, I was totally addicted to sex, masturbation, and pornography. It was in that broken condition, during my junior year of college that Christ found me. We sometimes tend to think that addictions simply vanish when we become new creations in Christ, but that's not usually how it works. After my conversion, as I've mentioned, I continued to struggle for another 2-3 years. One thing did change, though; I began to experience the conviction of the Holy Spirit. I tried unsuccessfully to get rid of all my pornography, but still the images played over and over in my mind. No magazines or videos were needed. Hundreds of hours of fantasy material had already been logged over the years.

As my sin and desires took me deeper, I began to struggle with thoughts that I might be homosexual. When I think back now, it seems that the beginning may have been the sexual abuse I experienced from my cousin at around eight or nine years of age. He awakened my sexuality at too young of an age, and with someone of the same sex. A few years later, I remember being attracted to a boy at basketball camp. I pushed it down and it didn't really resurface until college, *after my conversion to Christ*. Looking back, I still don't understand why it intensified upon becoming a Christian. Maybe it was the fruition of all the seeds I had planted or maybe God was bringing it to the surface so He could do something about it. As my same-sex desire grew, there was an enormous sense of shame and guilt that went with it. I was keenly aware of how some people must feel as they grapple with the reality that they might be gay. Though I fought, labored, and prayed, nothing changed. The desire only grew stronger, though it never progressed to same-sex activity.

My Story of Freedom

For three years I kept my struggle hidden from the world. I didn't want to be gay, but I felt like I had no choice in the matter. My story of freedom began with a sense of desperation and a longing to be free. It happened during a Thursday-night church service. One of my pastors was speaking about the downward spiral of sin from Romans 1 from Neil Anderson's book *The Bondage Breaker*. As he shared, my heart felt like it was beating out of my chest, and I knew the Holy Spirit wanted to do something profound in my life. Maybe the same thing is happening to you right now and God wants to deliver you from sexual brokenness. Just respond to what He is doing and follow His leading.

As the pastor closed the service, he gave an invitation that went something like this: "If you have a bondage in your life that you just can't seem to break, no matter what it is, just come to the front and begin to thank God for your freedom." I will never regret the decision to respond to that altar call. *Sometimes, taking a step of faith is the difference between freedom and bondage.* So I went up front. At first, I just whispered under my breath, "I praise you God for my freedom. Thank you for setting me free." But something on the inside told me it wasn't enough. Now I know it was the Holy Spirit saying, "Praise God with everything you've got!" So I did. I rejoiced, shouted praises, and jumped up and down. You may think it was just some crazy hyper-charismatic act, *but an undignified act of praise is actually a divine weapon.* It may make you and others feel uncomfortable, but God can use it to bring freedom to your life.

Praise Stills the Avenger

There is something about praise that silences and confounds the enemy. In the Old Testament, during battles, praise was a weapon and a strategy. In the book of Judges, when Israel was entering into battle, God instructed His people that Judah should go up first. *Judah* literally means, "praised" or "celebrated!"[4] Then in Joshua 6, Jericho was conquered when, after marching around the city for seven days, the Israelites blew their trumpets and shouted in praise to God! Praise is a weapon that, when employed, begets supernatural results:

> With *praises* from children and from tiny infants, you have built a fortress. *It makes your enemies silent,* and all who turn against you are left speechless. (Psalm 8:2 CEV)

As I humbled myself, surrendered to His will, and began to praise Him with all my might, my addiction to pornography and my same-sex attraction was instantaneously broken and I was free! It happened that quickly. It felt like a thousand-pound weight was lifted off each shoulder and a ball and chain was taken off my feet. Since that point, I have experienced lasting freedom from pornography and same-sex attraction. I am happily married to an incredible woman and have three beautiful children. I may, in the future, release a book sharing my story in more detail but the bottom line was this: *God had to do something supernatural in order to overcome sexual brokenness.*

My point in telling my story is not to present some new formula or theology, nor am I minimizing other people's stories that haven't had the same outcome. It's simply that – *it's my story.* You may not believe or like it, or maybe it gives you hope. I also want you to know, *I'm not condemning you.* I know what it's like to struggle with sexual brokenness. Some people have same-sex attraction (SSA) from a very young age and no matter what they do can't seem to overcome it. For some, it may never go away. Regardless of whether people are born that way or not (I'm not an expert in this area), there is something I believe at the core of my being that is true for every person in every generation: *There is freedom in Christ from all forms of sexual brokenness!* I'm not talking about "reparative therapy" or "praying it away." Freedom could involve life-long celibacy or deliverance from SSA, similar to mine. Deliverance seems far less common for most, yet it's not beyond God's capacity. Remember, nothing is impossible with God (see Luke 1:37). Either way, it can still be a long and slow process to maintain victory through accountability and guardrails. However He chooses to bring freedom, God will give you the grace to walk it out each day.

The Spirit of Baal

I believe one of the key contributors to our sex-crazed society is the spirit of Baal. Satan doesn't use new tactics; he uses the same ones he has always used. The children of Israel struggled with Baal worship through most of their history. Baal, the sun god, was the supreme god of the Canaanites. Human victims were sacrificed to him in times of plague or trouble. The victim was usually the firstborn and was generally burnt alive.[5] Listen to some of the traits common in Baal worship:

- Sexual Perversion
- Homosexuality
- Prostitution
- Violence and death
- Divorce
- Covenant breaking
- Racial strife

- Unfaithfulness
- Self-mutilation and cutting[6]

There is a day fast approaching when there will be another Elijah/Baal showdown—when the prophets of God confront the prophets of Baal (see 1 Kings 18). On that day, the Elijahs of God, the forerunners who are preparing the way for the return of the Lord, will issue a challenge to God's people like that of Elijah to the children of Israel: "How long will you falter between two opinions? If the Lord is God, follow Him: but if Baal, follow him" (1 Kings 18:21). In that day, God will answer by fire, the people of God will return to Him and Baal and his prophets will be defeated.

The State of Things

This issue of sexual perversion, immorality, and sexual addiction is prevalent in every realm of society and in every type of person. Douglass Weiss, a counselor with degrees in both divinity and psychology, said, "Wherever I am... and no matter what the denomination, at least half of the men in the church admit to being sexually addicted." Based on his experience, "The clergy don't differ that much from the general population—between a third to half."[7] It is a 97-billion-dollar-a-year industry worldwide and 13-billion-dollar-a-year industry in the United States alone. To give us some perspective, consider that twelve billion dollars is more than Google, Microsoft, Apple, Amazon, EBay, Yahoo!, Netflix, and EarthLink combined. It is more than all the pro sports teams combined make in a year. On top of that, three billion dollars a year is made on child pornography throughout the world.[8] We should be weeping and crying out to God over this.

Why is sexuality so twisted? The enemy seeks to provide a cheap imitation of the things of God by twisting, perverting, and counterfeiting.

What Does God Think About Sex?

This statement may surprise some, but God loves sex. He

created it for our enjoyment and for the procreation of godly offspring within the confines of marriage between a man and a woman. Let's look at some Scriptures:

> For this reason a man shall leave his father and his mother, and be joined to his wife; and they shall become one flesh. And the man and his wife were both naked and were not ashamed. (Genesis 2:24-25 NASB)

> Let marriage be held in honor (esteemed worthy, precious, of great price, and especially dear) in all things. And thus let the marriage bed be undefiled (kept undishonored); for God will judge and punish the unchaste [all guilty of sexual vice] and adulterous. (Hebrews 13:4 AMP)

There was no distortion at the time God created sexuality. It was meant for Adam and Eve to experience pleasure and to produce godly offspring. Sex is a wonderful gift when practiced in the context that God created it for—marriage! When practiced as prescribed by God, there is no shame, no guilt, no sexually transmitted disease (unless one partner comes into the relationship with a disease already), and no emotional wounding (in a normal, healthy sex life).

When we get into fornication or sex outside of marriage, it wounds us. The Bible tells us that when people have sex, they become *one flesh* (Genesis 2:24). Although oneness is meant for marriage, it applies outside of marriage as well. Sex produces a union, a bond, and an intimate connection. I've heard it called a "soul tie." When we are sexually active and the relationship doesn't work out, it's like taking two things that are intertwined with superglue and tearing them apart; it wounds and damages. God sets up boundaries, not to withhold good things from us, but to protect us and keep our lives from unnecessary pain and brokenness. He is a good God Father who wants to give us good things. Such is the case with sex.

In the world's eyes, everything goes. The world says it's OK to experiment with the same sex, look at a little pornography, switch partners, or live with a person before getting married. After all, the reasoning goes we've got to find out if we are compatible with each other. I don't believe we have to live with someone to know them, however. If you go through the right steps and processes, you can know someone very well. If the "chemistry" is right in all the other ways and there is physical attraction as well; the chemistry will probably be right in the bedroom too! The world will say it's OK to have sex with someone as long as we love him or her, but what is love? Far more than just a feeling, love is a commitment and a choice to be expressed in a covenant. The world would have us follow our feelings wherever they may lead us, but sex is a gift to be shared in the life-long covenant of marriage. Call me prudish, but I choose to believe the Bible.

Ladies, I can tell you with some level of certainty that when a man gets everything he wants outside of the covenant of marriage, he will be hard-pressed to marry you. Why get married when you have all the benefits of marriage with no formal commitment?

What Is a Covenant?

A covenant is a binding agreement with our spouse and with God that is not to be taken lightly. The concept of covenant is a practice used in cultures all over the world, usually taken with the intertwining of blood or in the case of marriage, sexual intercourse. People who understand this wouldn't think of breaking it. A covenant is different than a contract. In a contract, two parties agree on obligations they will fulfill as a part of the contract. In covenant, two parties are willingly binding themselves together and agreeing to live for the good of the other. Although I'm not going to go deep into covenant in this book, I would recommend doing some reading on this subject. I have included some resource recommendations at the end of the chapter.

How can we overcome sexual temptation, addiction and lust? In the next sections, we will discuss this for both men and women. My record has not been perfect, but the Lord has given me significant victory in this area.

How Men Can Overcome Sexual Temptation

In this section, I will address men specifically. Ladies, it's fine for you to read this section, too. It will help you grow in your understanding of men. Several of these principles also work regardless of your gender. So women, don't tune out!

You Need a Heart Change

I want to be careful not to simply provide a list of do's and don'ts as we talk about overcoming sexual temptation and addiction. *You don't need another list of dos and don'ts when it comes to overcoming sexual temptation; what you need is a heart change.* You can't do this on our own, especially if you are addicted. Admitting you have a problem is the first step. You must become "poor in spirit" (expressing that you are helpless without God, see Matthew 5:3) and express your deficiency and His all-sufficiency. We are weak; He is strong (see 2 Corinthians 12:10). We must allow Him to be strong in our lives. The rest of the principles after this will help you maintain freedom, but they won't bring freedom. Remember from a previous chapter, grace is not only the power that saves us; it's the power that frees us and keeps us! It starts with allowing God to deal with the heart. God's grace and mercy empower us to overcome temptation and remain free from addiction.

Make a Covenant with Your Eyes

First, men you are visually-oriented and God made you that way. Sometimes it feels like a curse, but God meant it to be a blessing.

Like Job, we need to make a covenant with our eyes "I made a covenant with my eyes not to look lustfully at a girl" (Job 31:1 NIV). For a man, it all starts with your eyes. That means you must learn to have self-control over where your eyes land. Let's be real; you are going to notice women. To simply notice a beautiful woman, whether dressed appropriately or not, isn't a sin. To be walking through a grocery store and see a magazine cover that's placed strategically in front of you is not sin. That's unavoidable. But to dwell on and fantasize about a woman is a different issue altogether.

The eyes are the gateway to your mind, which makes up part of our soul. *What we behold, we become.* As we dwell on an image with our eyes, that image becomes embedded in the mind. That is where the real battle begins. If we can stop an image from being embedded in our mind, we have won the battle. To notice a woman or a picture is one thing; to take several glances because we like what we see is another.

Guys, I know it's hard. I've been there and still struggle myself at times, but we must learn by God's grace to have self-control in this area and look away. Although I don't know where it came from, some refer to it as, "bouncing your eyes." It's not just some legalistic practice; it's a covenant with your eyes that can keep you from falling into sin! Once an image is embedded in your mind, and you begin to lust over it, action is almost inevitable – masturbation, fantasizing, pornography, or adultery. It usually goes from mind to reality. Martin Luther is generally credited for saying, "You can't keep the birds from flying over your head, but you can prevent them from building a nest in your hair!" This is so true. You will notice things, and you can't stop a thought that suddenly enters your mind, but you can decide what to do with it.

Be Accountable to Someone

Therefore, confess your sins to one another, and pray for one another so that you may be healed. The

> effective prayer of a righteous man can accomplish much. (James 5:15 NASB)

> He who conceals his transgressions [sins] will not prosper, But he who confesses and forsakes them will find compassion. (Proverbs 28:13 NASB)

Since God delivered me from sexual addiction, accountability has been a critical part of keeping my victory. Once we gain victory, we have to keep taking ground. If not, it's easy to lose our victory. One of the ways we keep advancing is through accountability with someone of the same sex who has a level of victory in the same area. It takes humility to maintain accountability. Confessing your sins on a consistent basis is not an easy, comfortable, or enjoyable thing. In fact, sometimes it's rather embarrassing! Although it's difficult, it's well worth the freedom it brings.

Let me give you an example. I use a program on my computer called Covenant Eyes. It sends a weekly e-mail to three people of my choice listing the websites I have visited in the past week. One of the people who receive that e-mail is my wife. Just knowing that, if I look at pornography my wife will know, immediately deters me from going any further. Yes, my ultimate desire for purity is to please the God who loves me and died for me. How better to do that than staying accountable to a visible person? Accountability is a way of humbling ourselves. The Scripture says that when we do this, God will lift us up (see James 4:10).

> If we say we have fellowship with him while we walk in darkness, we lie and do not practice the truth. But if we walk in the light, as he is in the light, *we have fellowship with one another, and the blood of Jesus his Son cleanses us from all sin.* (1 John 1:6-7)

Get Radical

> If your hand or your foot causes you to stumble, cut it off and throw it from you; it is better for you to enter life crippled or lame, than to have two hands or two feet and be cast into the eternal fire. If your eye causes you to stumble, pluck it out and throw it from you. It is better for you to enter life with one eye, than to have two eyes and be cast into the fiery hell. (Matthew 18:8-9 NASB)

If this passage were true in a literal sense, there would be lots of one-eyed, one-handed people walking around! The revelation of this passage is that we need to *radically amputate any source of sin in our lives!* Sin is like a tumor. It seeks to attack us, spread like cancer, and completely overtake us. We need to treat it as such and attack it with force to dislodge it. Amputating sin in our lives is only part of the answer. We fight from a place of victory over sin (see 1 Corinthians 15:57-58 and Col. 2:14-15). In Christ, we are complete and have every spiritual blessing for life and godliness (see 2 Peter 1:3). As we grow in these profound truths, we find ourselves sinning less and less and becoming more and more like Christ.

Here are some examples of radically amputating sin in the area of sexual immorality. These are radical measures, but worth it for your freedom:

- Burn or get rid of any sources of pornography and lust
- Give up your computer—sell it, give it to a friend for a season, cancel the Internet, or if you must have it for work, put an Internet filter or accountability program on it
- Cancel your credit cards
- Get an accountability partner you can call anytime and get together with regularly for confession and encouragement;
- Don't watch TV alone late at night. Get rid of your TV, cable, or DVD player if need be
- Admit you have a problem and seek help
- Get some good Christian counseling if you have a problem with sexual addiction. It's not just going to go away. Your freedom is worth it.

Many of these are preventative measures, or "motes" if you will. But I found that some of them are absolutely necessary to maintaining your freedom, especially in the beginning of overcoming a sexual addiction. The enemy will try to get you to stumble at every turn.

My family moved into our first home a little before Christmas in 2006. On Christmas Eve morning, I was in my new home office. I was so excited; I had prayed for a home with an office so I would have a private place to connect with Jesus. Yet every time I tried, it seemed like there was some hindrance or distraction. It felt like God's presence was nowhere to be found. I noticed the lights were very dim in my office, so finally I got up enough unction to get a small ladder, take out a ceiling tile, and see why it was so dim. As I poked my head into the drop ceiling, I saw several pornographic DVDs in the ceiling from the previous owners. I quickly took them down and had a Christmas Eve bonfire! We immediately prayed over the house and anointed it with oil. Since that time, I have had no trouble at all connecting with Jesus in my office!

Another time, I was traveling several hours away to preach on a Sunday morning. Most of the time when I traveled, I stayed with a family from the church, but on this occasion the church decided to put me up in a hotel. Again, I was having a problem with the light. The lamp in my room wasn't working at all, so I decided to try a different outlet. When I pulled out the dresser to find another outlet, I found several pornographic magazines tucked behind the dresser! I immediately stuffed them into a bag and took them out to the attendant, told him what had happened, and asked him to get rid of them. Eventually, I asked him to switch my room. I didn't want to be thinking all night about what had taken place in that room.

Temptation and Accountability

Once we gain a level of victory over our besetting sins, it's not that we are immune to sin, but we will have gotten into the practice of resisting temptation effectively. We are able to listen to and obey the Holy Spirit's promptings to overcome sin. In the beginning, we must cut off the source of the sin by getting radical. Over time, we will probably be able to reinstate some of those things we had to cut off in the beginning—things like television and Internet, but *we will never get beyond the need for good accountability and safeties! It's in your weak moments that these guardrails do what they are designed to do.*

Safeties

Every person needs to have what I would call "safeties" for those exposed or weak places in their lives. For people who are dealing with any type of addiction, this is doubly true. A safety is like a breaker or a fuse inside an electric panel. A fuse, when it's going to overheat or is overtaxed, trips so that the system cannot be overloaded. If overloaded, the system could start on fire or malfunction in a potentially dangerous way. *In our lives, a safety is a practice set in place for the purpose of guarding us in times of trouble and short-circuiting any potentially damaging temptations.* Safeties short-circuit the sin process, and many times stop the momentum of sin enough to where we stop, rethink it, and go another direction. We can't trust ourselves to always do what's right. We need to have safeties built into our lives that keep us from faltering when we are tempted. Some examples would be:

- Call a friend in your time of need.
- Put a filter on your computer or use a program such as Covenant Eyes to keep stay accountable. If using a filter, let a friend or your spouse set the passwords so you can't circumvent them.
- Have a weekly accountability time with a trusted friend where you can share your sinful shortcomings and pray for one another.

As I already mentioned, lust is an exposed place for me. It's an area where I need to have safeties. That's why I have filters or passwords on every computer we own. That's why I keep the remote nearby ready to flip to PBS or another channel when a provocative commercial comes on.

I once watched Oprah Winfrey interview the former the pastor of New Life Church in Colorado Springs and leader of the National Association of Evangelicals, Ted Haggard. It was a very sad story. He was outspoken about marriage between one man and one woman and yet ended up falling into an adulterous homosexual relationship and using drugs. Apparently, he did seek counsel from some of his spiritual leaders about some of the homosexual feelings and compulsions he was having, some of whom said he should "further immerse himself in church work."[9] That was poor advice. Doing more work will never fill the void in our souls. Ted admitted in the interview that he wished he had counseling for these compulsions years before. Without minimizing or trivializing the problem, the right safeties may have prevented this from happening. While he was getting help for some of the root issues, even if the same sex attraction persisted, bringing the problem into the light and fighting the good fight of faith may have been enough to maintain victory and honor the covenant he had made to his wife. Thankfully, his family is still together and there has been much healing that has taken place, according to Ted.

It's impossible to hide things forever. Jesus will only allow you to live a hypocritical life for so long. It is for your own good that your sin must come into the light. If you deal with it in private, it doesn't have to become public. God doesn't want to shame you publically; He wants to deal with it privately and have you willingly bring it into the light as you do whatever is necessary to root it out of your life. By "private," I don't necessarily mean alone. This should include trusted confidants that you can share everything with. One form of God's love and discipline is to convict people of sin. If we don't respond to His loving discipline, it will grow more intense. One way or the other, our sin will come out.

When it comes to leadership, God would rather heal us *before* we ever get to a position of influence so it doesn't have to surface once we have influence. In order for Him to do so, you must deal with your sin regularly and often. Even when your sin does surface, God's intention is always love. He is more interested in the eternal state of our souls than He is in our career or ministry.

One of my primary prayers over the years has been, *Lord, don't bring me to a place where my character can't keep me.* In other words, if my character isn't ready, then I'm not ready! I want my character to be developed enough to handle the pressure of the place of influence God has for me. It may be a slower path, but at the end of my life, I would rather it be said that I finished well. *My desire is that those closest to me respect me most.*

After seeing how many ministers have stumbled in the area of sexual temptation, Billy Graham decided never to be alone with a woman other than his wife. I have adopted this practice as well, even before reading about Billy Graham. I don't want to give any place for an attachment to form with a woman other than my wife. This is what I call a "safety." Safeties involve *examining our weak places and marking out boundaries for our lives!*

What About Masturbation?

There are wide and varying views on masturbation within Christian circles, and I'm not going to be comprehensive about it. I believe the best thing we can do is look at it in the light of biblical principles rather than a black and white, right or wrong issue. Masturbation is not mentioned anywhere in the Bible. The terms most used are *sexual immorality* and *fornication.* There are also other lists of prohibited sexual acts mentioned in the Scripture. (See my list of some Scriptures at the end of the chapter.)

Most often, masturbation is associated with lustful thoughts and fantasies, many times fueled by pornographic images. If this is the case for you then it is sin by virtue of association. Most likely, if masturbation is a part of your life, so are fantasies and impure thoughts. If not, you are one of the few. Although it's possible to masturbate without lustful thoughts, it's probably not the norm. Jesus gave us this standard, "But I say to you that everyone who looks at a woman with lustful intent has already committed adultery with her in his heart" (Matthew 5:28). Jesus doesn't just want us to be pure in our actions, but in our minds, hearts, and desires as well.

If you are one of the few people who don't fantasize when you masturbate, then you need to be the judge of whether or not it is sin. Why are you doing it? How does it make you feel afterward? Does it make you feel guilty and shameful? Does it produce good fruit or bad fruit? Does it cause you to focus inwardly in a selfish way? Does it affect those around you by changing your mood or demeanor? Is it used to "medicate" or alleviate another area in your life (stress, relational tension, boredom, and so forth)? Are you unable to resist the temptation to do it? Are you using it in place of pursuing sexual intimacy with your wife? If any of these things are true, it's probably something that needs to be surrendered to God.

Please don't misunderstand me. It's not always as easy as saying, "just get over it" or "just stop it." As I stated before, I was taught about masturbation around age eight. For me, it became an escape from frustration, stress, anxiety, and an unstable home situation. After I became a Christian, I began to feel guilty and shameful about it, especially when tied to fantasies and pornography. Christians need to be turning to Jesus rather than other things, whether masturbation, eating, television, fantasy, pornography, or any other potentially damaging or unfruitful thing. I know how hard it is to stop, especially if it has become second nature to you. Although I was delivered instantly from the addiction to pornography, masturbation didn't just go away. It's been a slow, steady plod.

If this is a struggle for you, renewing your mind and learning how to rely on Jesus to lead you out of temptation is a must. You must take everything back to the cross of Christ, where He accomplished it all. *Your freedom is found at the cross.* It comes by consistent revelation of your deficiency and His sufficiency and learning to access His power, strength, and grace day-by-day and minute-by-minute. If masturbation is not linked with lust, search your heart as to why you are doing it. Have an accountability partner. Confess it when it is tied to lust. Pay attention to how it makes you feel. Don't demonize the act or yourself. People often try to lump it into "sexual immorality," but if it's not linked with lustful thoughts, it's hard to make a case for that, and self-condemnation and self-loathing won't help you overcome it. Condemnation will lead you further away from God, but the conviction of the Holy Spirit will lead you to God. Although it's not specifically mentioned in the Bible, if it's not from a place of faith, it is sin (see Romans 14:23).

Here are some things that have helped me with masturbation. These are things that may help you overcome temptation, but for lasting freedom, you must go deeper by letting Jesus show you the root. For me, much of the root for my sin habits is control. When I am not in control of something or a situation, it causes me to want to turn to other things like anger or lust in an attempt to gain control. We must let Him work on us from the inside out to get to the root of our sin and bring true freedom.

The Three-Minute Temptation Buster

Bruce Wilkinson, in his book, *Spiritual Breakthroughs,* talks about how he made a dramatic breakthrough in his understanding of sin. Feeling at times seemingly overwhelmed by temptation, he wondered if there was no real answer for victory. Here is what happened:

> When I discovered that my emotions right before every temptation were distressed to some level and I was actually seeking comfort, I asked God to show me

another way to find it. That's when I remembered the promise of Jesus to send someone to be my personal comforter! Listen to what He told His disciples in the upper room: "And I will pray the Father, and he shall give you another Comforter..." (John 14:16-17). I wondered what would happen if I specifically asked for this comfort in times of temptation. I decided to try. My simple request went like this: "Dear Holy Spirit, You've been sent to me to be my personal Comforter. I am in desperate need of comfort. I don't want to sin. Please comfort me. In Jesus' name, Amen." At first nothing happened. How discouraged and defeated I felt at that moment. But then I slowly became aware of something—I felt comforted! I didn't know exactly when I was comforted, I only knew that I was—and that my soul felt soothed and no longer in pain. When I turned back toward that temptation, I discovered that it had miraculously slithered back into the darkness, far away from my senses. I was free. Instead of finding it hard not to sin at that moment, I found it easy because the need to sin had faded, and my heart was surrounded with satisfaction and warmth. I've prayed to my Comforter many times since, and I've discovered two immutable truths (1) the Holy Spirit always—and I mean always—completes His responsibility in my heart (2) He always gives me His comfort within 3 minutes, though I can never put my finger on the moment when He does. Now I call this prayer for comfort my "Three-Minute Temptation Buster."[10]

Exercise

Exercise seems to take away some stored-up energy that may fuel using masturbation as a "release." Exercise is also known to release *endorphins* (small protein molecules that are produced by cells in your nervous system and other parts of your body). Endorphins have been shown to "control persistent pain, control the craving for chocolate (I don't know if I like that one) and potentially addictive substances, control feelings of stress and frustration, regulate the production of growth and sex hormones, and reduce symptoms associated with eating disorders." They produce a "natural high" and are also released through other activities, such as sex, meditation, laughter, eating spicy foods, acupuncture, and chiropractic adjustments![11]

Immediately Switch Gears to Do Something Else

Normally you would be alone when tempted with masturbation. Try immediately switching gears and just go do something else. Take a walk, a jog, run an errand, or take the dog for a walk. For other helpful hints, refer back to the list earlier in the chapter about overcoming sexual temptation.

Be Sensitive to the Holy Spirit

Nothing can replace sensitivity to the Holy Spirit. Jesus, who "was in every way tempted as we are, yet without sin," promised to give us a way of escape when we are tempted (see Hebrews 4:15 and 1 Corinthians 10:13). He also taught us to pray, "...lead us out of temptation" (see Matthew 6:10), which means He is offering His help. If we are sensitive to the Holy Spirit, He will lead us out of temptation *every time*. Take advantage of it!

For the Ladies (Guys Are Welcome to Read)

Ladies are not exempt from sexual temptation. According to studies, "28% of those admitting to sexual addiction are women."[12] Women may not be as visually driven as men, but they can still struggle with sexual impurity and addiction. Some good books have been written the subject that specifically target women struggling with sexual addiction. I have listed these at the end of the chapter.

In this section, I want to talk about a few of these issues as they relate to women. Don't worry, it won't all be from a man's perspective! I recruited my wife to help me on this issue. Although her opinions don't represent all women, it will provide a woman's perspective on the matter. I will present it in a question/answer type format. My wife readily admits that she is not speaking for all women, but is simply sharing things from her experience and perspective.

Question: How are women sexually tempted?

Gina: Women aren't usually sexually tempted in all the same ways men are. I have no personal experience with pornography, so I can't speak to that. That's not to say men or images of men can't be visually stimulating.

Kent: Like Johnny Depp or Fabio?

Gina: Physical attractiveness isn't the first thing we usually pay attention to. We don't usually look at an attractive guy and say, "Whew, I would like to hop in bed with him!" Women want love, acceptance, and attention. We want to know we are cherished and treasured. Sexual temptation can certainly play into that scenario. For a young, single Christian woman, if a guy is paying a lot of attention to her and making her feel special, like she is the only one, it would be very easy to be tempted. It may be even more tempting if she didn't have a good father/daughter relationship or didn't have many positive male role models in her life.

Question: How are a woman's emotions tied to sexual temptation?

Gina: Again, I'm not speaking to women who have had significant emotional wounding or trauma, as I have no experience with this. They may be dealing with sexual issues in a whole different way. Women are complex.

It goes back to love and acceptance. Temptation can increase when you feel attractive or when someone is telling you they love you and you are the most beautiful women in the world. If you are in a relationship with that man already, it's hard not to melt into his arms at that point. Barring other circumstances, like emotional wounding or having too much to drink at a party, I think sexual temptation is usually tied to relationship for a woman.

Question: What can women do to guard against becoming emotionally attached too soon in a relationship?

Gina: Obviously, in the context of a relationship, if a man is pursuing sexual intimacy outside of marriage, you need to find a new man! Check your own motives in the relationship. Why do you want to be in this relationship? You should also check the man's motives. How well do you know him? What are his intentions with you? If you have a godly male role model in your life, get his perspective. You should be asking these questions sooner rather than later.

When I was eighteen, I just wanted someone to like me and care about me, so I was swayed by anyone who showed me a little bit of attention. The only thing is, they usually ended up being the wrong type of guy. Nobody told me to be careful about this. You need make boundaries for your relationships. Try not to spend a lot of time alone with a man, but rather spend time in a group context. It might sound prudish, but our temptations are a lot stronger than we think. This works whether we are in a relationship or not. When we do get into a relationship, it's even more important to sit down and discuss boundaries. You may even want to include a married couple in on that conversation. Boundaries should be clear. It's better to err on the side of caution. When Kent and I were in this place in life, some of the boundaries we made were not clear enough. Although we remained pure, we had to backtrack at times. Once you cross those lines, it becomes even more difficult to go back.

Question: You were a virgin when you got married. What kept you from having sex before marriage?

Gina: Even though I was a rebellious teen, I felt really convicted that sex before marriage was wrong. Like many in my generation, it wasn't really talked about but only hinted at that it was very wrong outside of marriage. I also had a lot of fear of the consequences. I was really afraid of having a baby or getting an STD. It was totally God's grace! I also felt like I would be a disappointment to God and to my future husband. Right or wrong, I felt like I didn't want to have to explain to my husband that I had slept with other people. If you have had sex before marriage, God can totally redeem you. I believe that, but it's better if you don't have to go through the pain that accompanies sex outside of marriage.

Kent: Just for the record, I was one of those people who had more than a few sexual partners before marriage and before Christ. By the time I walked down the altar, knowing I had led my soon-to-be wife in purity, I felt like a new man. I am a testimony to the fact that Christ can totally redeem a person.

Question: Are there any things you can share that would be helpful to women in overcoming sexual temptation?

Gina: The basic point I want to get across is that if you are having issues in any area, specifically with lust and temptation, your heart needs to be changed by the Lord. That is the only way you can find freedom from the issues you are facing. As your heart is changed by the Lord, your actions will be out of love and obedience for Him. This is a heart-level issue. Most likely, you are using sex/lust to try to satisfy some broken or empty place in your heart. As far as practical measures go, I think accountability is important. Have someone you can be honest with—someone who can pray for you, keep you accountable, and challenge you. Also, have boundaries in place, as I referred to previously.

Question: How does modesty play into the equation for women overcoming sexual temptation?

Gina: There is a quote from Shannon Ethridge, who wrote *Every Young Woman's Battle.* She said, "Whatever bait you use determines the type of fish you catch." If you want a godly man, you need to dress like you want a godly man. Understand that men are visual. What they see is very important. I'm not saying you can't be stylish. I love fashion. But there is a way to go about it without drawing unnecessary attention.

Kent: As an aside, Gina is one of the most fashionable, but tasteful, people I know!

Gina: When I think of immodesty, I think of being able to see things in public that you should only see in private, such as your cleavage, stomach, or buttocks via extremely short or tight clothing. You know what's inappropriate because you look at other women and say, "That's inappropriate!" If you don't really know if something is immodest or not, ask a friend who has some modesty or maybe even your brother or your dad!

Kent: As a man of God, when I see a woman dressed inappropriately either on TV or on the street, I am saddened. I think to myself, *They are so beautiful, and they think they need to dress that way to get attention.* In the spirit of full disclosure, it is also very hard not to keep looking. It takes a lot of discipline and help from the Holy Spirit. Job said, "I made a covenant with my eyes, not to look with lust at a young woman." (Job 31:1 NLT).

Gina: A godly man wants a godly woman. If you are dressed in such a way that men ogle you, you will attract men who want to sleep with you! As a Christian woman, you are also causing your brother to stumble. Now understand, men can still take a beautiful, modest women and undress her in their minds, but that's their problem. It's perfectly fine to look nice. I like to look nice when I leave the house. If your motive when you leave the house is to attract unnecessary attention, your motives are off and there may be deeper issues at play. It's an identity issue. You probably don't know your standing in Christ. You are a child of God. The problem is identity.

Here are some tips for being modest:

- If you are wearing a low v-neck, wear a coordinating tank top under it or layers. You can still look very stylish this way!
- If you have really tight clothes, wear something over them. For example, with tight tops, you can put a jacket or cardigan over them. With very tight jeans (like leggings),

you can wear a longer shirt over them.
- If your pants are so tight you have to lay down and have your friend pull up the zipper with a pair of pliers, they are too tight!
- Ask a modest friend or a trusted family member if you're not sure.

Question: Any last things you want to say?

Gina: We are stewards of our bodies that God gave us; they are temples. I feel like God wants us to have integrity and wants us to present ourselves in a way that brings glory and honor to Him. Our highest motive should be to please Him. If our heart motive is right, the outside will reflect that. Also, I just want to close with this: It's difficult but possible to stay sexually pure in this generation. Stay close to the Lord, live in community with others, and don't give up in a weak moment only to live with regrets.

Discussion Questions

Split up into same-sex groups of 3-5 people.

1. What are some of your struggles concerning sexuality?
2. Do you have accountability? If not, find someone by next week and ask the people in this group to keep you accountable! I strongly encourage you to find someone who has a level of victory and will get in your face if need be.
3. Do you need to "get radical" and cut off any sources of sin? If so, what are the specific sources of sin you need to cut off? (Examples: get rid of any pornographic materials, cancel Internet or cable, cancel credit cards, and so forth.) Share these specific things with your accountability partner and give that person permission to ask about these things.
4. Are you in an immoral relationship? (Pre-marital sexual activity, homosexuality, and the like.) If so, the relationship needs to be ended. Share this with your accountability partner and ask this person to keep you accountable to the

proper action.

5. Do you have any safeties set up for yourself? If not, write down a list of safeties you are going to put in place. Give a list to your accountability partner as well. It's important not to think of these as rules and regulations, but as boundaries by which God wants to keep you safe.

6. Do you need to see your pastor or possibly even a professional counselor about any of your issues? Your freedom is worth it!

Recommended Books

Appendix C: Keys to Freedom: Overcoming Sexual Addiction
Not Even a Hint by Joshua Harris
Every Man's Battle by Steven Arterburn
The Bondage Breaker by Neil Anderson
The Final Freedom by Douglass Weiss
Every Woman's Battle by Shannon Ethridge
Passion and Purity by Elisabeth Elliot

Web Resources

www.settingcaptivesfree.org—This website has many 60-day programs for sexual addictions. Try "The Way of Purity." It is supposed to be excellent! Enrollment is *free,* and they provide you with an accountability partner!

www.firesofdarkness.com/index.htm—This site is very helpful.

www.xxxchurch.com—This site is a bit edgy, maybe too edgy for some things, but has some great resources, including "X-3 watch," which is a free internet accountability program.

www.covenanteyes.com—Sends out a weekly update to your choice of three different people. They also have an Internet filter that goes along with the program. I personally use this program. Although it does the same thing as the XXX Church program, it seems to be much more reliable.

www.purelifeministries.org—They have a recovery center in Kentucky.

Scripture Verses About Sex and Sexuality

Leviticus 18:6-24
Song of Solomon—the whole book!
Proverbs 5:17-23
Matthew 5:27-30
Romans 1:26-27
1 Corinthians 6:9-20
Galatians 5:16-21
Ephesians 4:19-24
Ephesians 5:3-5
1 Thessalonians 4:3-8
Hebrews 13:4
1 Timothy 1:9-10
Revelation 21:8

Meditation Verse

The temptations in your life are no different from what others experience. And God is faithful. He will not allow the temptation to be more than you can stand. When you are tempted, He will show you a way out so that you can endure. (1 Corinthians 10:13 NLT)

CHAPTER 10

CHOOSING THE RIGHT RELATIONSHIPS

In this chapter, I will talk about both romantic relationships and friendship relationships. Specifically, I want to help you know how to choose the right relationships. Let's talk about the one everyone is thinking about first—romantic relationships!

Romantic Relationships

Since the beginning of time, romantic relationships have been at the forefront of human existence. I have already shared about sex, so in this chapter we will limit ourselves to other aspects of romantic relationships and some principles that will help you choose the right spouse.

What H. Jackson Brown, Jr. said is very true: "Marry the right person. This one decision will determine 90% of your happiness or misery."[1] There are many things to account for when making a decision about a life-long mate. Obviously, this is not a decision you should take lightly. Maybe you are just "playing the field," looking for the right person and testing people out right now. I think there are better ways to do this. There are lots of great books on this subject, so I won't go into all the details, but I will touch on some principles that have proved helpful.

This is my story of choosing the right relationship after choosing a bunch of wrong ones. By the time Christ saved me during my junior year of college, my view of women and relationships was very distorted. I had had many different sexual partners and I had a poor model of marriage in my home as well. When I became a follower of Christ, I carried my faulty views and strongholds in with me.

There was one young lady who I will refer to as Jamie. She

was a very good friend of mine during college. Shortly after my conversion to Christ, I was lying in bed one morning when suddenly a rather obnoxious and loud thought (which I took to be the voice of God) came to me. It said, "One day you will be a preacher, and you will marry Jamie!" The first thing out of my mouth was, "Nooooooooo!" The preacher part was fine, but the reason I shouted, "Nooooooooo," was not because there was anything wrong with Jamie. In fact, she was one of the most intelligent, upstanding young ladies I knew and an awesome friend who challenged me and helped me grow in my newfound faith. The reason I shouted, "Nooooooooo," was because I just couldn't ever see her as my wife.

Satan comes disguised as an angel of light (see 2 Cor. 11:14), often using part truths and familiar things to trip us up, especially in the area of relationships. At one point, we both came together for a discussion and decided God had called us to be married. There was just one problem; I had absolutely no physical attraction toward her whatsoever. Maybe you think that sounds vain, but when you are thinking about spending the rest of your life with someone, that's a problem! In my immaturity, I thought it was an obedience issue and God was going to "make me" marry this young lady! I struggled with this for two years until an older man said, "I don't think God would make you marry someone you aren't attracted to."

Over time, I came to the realization that I had been deceived. God wasn't asking me to marry Jamie at all. What a relief! When I finally got up the guts to tell her my feelings, she disagreed. She still felt that we were supposed to be married. Thank God I didn't go too far with that one, for both our sakes! Although we never crossed any lines physically or sexually, the relationship was damaged beyond repair, and I lost one of my best friends from college. I tried several times over next few years to mend things with no success.

Life-Saving Principles

1) Find out what those close to you think about your relationship. It could save your life! Chances are, if all or most of the important people in your life are cautioning you about a relationship, you would be wise to pay attention. Sometimes we are the only one who can't see what's really happening.

My office used to be located on the campus of a Bible school. I can't tell you how many times I heard a young person say, "God has spoken to me that so-and-so is to be my mate," only to find out the other person didn't feel the same way. Newsflash: if the other person doesn't feel the same way, you are out of luck! It could be a timing issue, or it could just be a mistake. At that point, you need to acknowledge that and move on.

As for Gina and me, we had been friends for several months when she wrote me a letter sharing her true feelings for me. She would say now that was a mistake.

2) Always let the man take the initiative. When Gina wrote me the letter, I was moving forward in my walk with Christ, but still had some major issues to resolve before having a healthy relationship. Among other things, I was struggling with a sexual addiction and my sexual identity. I liked her a lot, but knew I would hurt her if I jumped into a relationship at that time. After telling her I didn't feel that we were to move the relationship to the next level, she was hurt by my answer, and over the next six months we drifted apart. In the meantime, God had begun to work powerfully in my life, and I had experienced a profound deliverance from my sexual addiction and the deception that I was homosexual.

Around that time, I heard Gina had been hanging out with another guy and I began to feel jealous. This is when I began to notice that my feelings for Gina went beyond friendship. A short while later during a time of prayer, I had a revelatory experience where I was confident that Gina was to be my bride. God gave me a love for her beyond what I could naturally conjure up and yes, I was also very attracted to her! I proceeded in a way that was a little abrupt, but it worked. I tend to be a direct person, so I called her on the phone and asked her if we could get together and talk. I laid it all out on the table. The first thing I said (after six months of awkwardness) was, "God has given me an incredible love for you, and I want to work towards marriage!" Gina was floored and didn't know what to say. She said she needed some time to think about it. Five days later, I was going crazy (though she had waited six months), so I called her and asked her if we could have coffee. She shared that she felt the same way and had for a long while, but had given it up to the Lord when I turned her down six months earlier. Six months later, we were engaged and then married nine months after that.

We have been married for over fifteen years now. Gina and I love each other very much, and we have a good relationship, but not without some rough patches. Bringing two lives together, both with baggage, is not an easy thing to do. Even when you know God has placed you together and you are both walking with God, it can be tough. I always tell people the two most difficult and most fulfilling things I have ever done in life so far are marriage and ministry! The enemy doesn't like either; that's why He attacks them so vehemently. A Christ-centered, close-knit marriage and family have the power to change lives and provide a picture of how Christ relates to His Church (see Ephesians 5:32). Just bring a broken generation around your family dinner table and see how they respond. This is ministry in its truest form. Nonetheless, Paul says that those who marry will have troubles in the flesh, both in the way of increased pressure during persecution and possible sorrows and troubles that will come when bringing two lives together.

> But if you do marry, you do not sin [in doing so], and if a virgin marries, she does not sin [in doing so]. Yet those who marry will have physical and earthly troubles, and I would like to spare you that. (1 Corinthians 7:28 AMP)

I'm certainly not trying to discourage marriage. It's a good thing, but it takes a lot of prayer, hard work, commitment, and a willingness to do whatever it takes to make it work. He who finds a wife finds a good thing (see Proverbs 18:22). My wife is such a blessing. She brings such a balance and joy to my life. At the same time, marriage is a crucial decision, and it is extremely important to make sure that you marry the right person!

Qualities to Look For In a Mate

Here are some qualities I came up with (in no particular order of importance) that Christians should be looking for in a potential mate. There are probably more comprehensive lists out there, but this should get you started.

1. Godliness—Hanging out in groups will give you a good idea about some of these things without the pressure of intimacy. Here are some questions to ask. Is this person:

- A Christian? If not, stop pursuing the relationship right away! (see 2 Corinthians 6:14 and Amos 3:3)
- Actively pursuing Christ? Does he or she seem to have a close relationship with Christ?
- Consistent fellowship with other believers and rooted in a local church?
- Submissive to authority in their life?

2. Integrity—This could be looked at in many ways, including: truthfulness, faithfulness, trustworthiness, and responsibility. You should pay attention to all these things. Does this person:

- Have a steady job?
- Follow through with commitments and promises?
- Tell the truth?
- Stay committed to beliefs and convictions? Do others recognize this?

3. Physical Attraction—I mentioned this element in my story about Jamie: I wasn't attracted to her in the way a husband should be attracted to his wife. Though this shouldn't be the only thing you look for in a mate, it is important. This is the person you plan on spending the rest of your life with, so you ought to be physically attracted to that person. But again, this should not be the *only* thing you are looking at either. Physical chemistry is only one aspect of a relationship.

4. Likeable and Compatible Personality—This person should be someone with whom you get along well and at least share some of the same interests, but not all. Interestingly enough, in Genesis 2:18, the Hebrew word for "help meet" or "helper" is *neged*, which can mean "a part opposite, counterpart, or other side."[71] Often times, though you may share some common interests, your strengths and weakness will be different from your spouse's in order to complement one another. This is a good thing, giving strength where you are weak, but it can also lead to friction. You will have to learn how to receive from your mate, value their differing perspective and gifts, and know that God placed you together to strengthen one another.

5. Same Values and Ideals—It's not that you have to agree with this person in every area, but on the major things you should have similar values—things like faith, core beliefs, calling, marriage, and children. Many people get into trouble when they marry someone of totally different values. For example, if one person has a core value that you are to rooted and planted in the body of Christ, serving and using your gifts and the other person believes faith is a personal thing to be lived out privately, what happens when you have children? The first person wants to find a community of faith and the other doesn't believe it's necessary. You must talk through these issues with a potential mate in order to see if you are compatible or if your difference in values is too large to overcome. It's also important to include other seasoned couples in some of these conversations.

Additionally, if you both are of faith in God, but one has a much different background and has very different traditions, this can make things difficult as well. I have seen this happen over and over, especially with women. Many women want to be married so badly that they let their desire for a mate overtake their common sense and wise counsel. They end up in a relationship with a lukewarm or unbelieving man, and it spells disaster! Young men and women, I don't care how attracted you are to the other person,–if that person is on a totally different spiritual wavelength, it's either bad timing or not a fit. The Scriptures are also clear that a believer should not be "yoked" to an unbeliever:

> Do not be unequally yoked with unbelievers. For what partnership has righteousness with lawlessness? Or what fellowship has light with darkness? What accord has Christ with Belial? Or what portion does a believer share with an unbeliever? (2 Corinthians 6:14-15 ESV)

This verse is not used in specific reference to marriage, but can certainly be applied. The word *yoked* means "to be bound up or walking in close fellowship or relationship." The picture is that of two different animals being yoked together for purposes of work (see Deuteronomy 22:10).[3] If one is out of step with the other or unequal in strength or size, they can't do the work effectively. It also refers to leaving one's own rank, order, or place to go into another.[4] In marriage, if one person is out of step or on a different page altogether, how can they walk together? *You will have heartache after heartache should you enter into a relationship with a person who is not of faith in Christ.* I can't stress this enough: wait for the person God has chosen for you and you will never regret it.

Let's go over a few other principles that will help you in relationships.

Dating vs. Courting

Dating or "playing the field" is overrated. My understanding of *dating* is this: to see, spend time, and experiment physically with different people in order to find the one that's right for you. Often in dating, you are "trying the person out" in order to find out if you are compatible. Many times it involves significant levels of intimacy. After all, you should find out if this person is going to work for you, right? In the world's system of values, this can even involve living together before marriage. Why do Christians listen to the world when it comes to dating? Statistics show that people who live together before marriage are less likely to get married, have a higher rate of divorce, and are unhappier when they do get married![5]

When I think of dating, a show called *The Bachelor* comes to mind. It's one guy, twelve ladies, and a whole lot of lust! This one man spends individual time with each woman, usually pursues intimate physical relationships with several of them and, who knows, may end up "getting lucky" with more than one (they don't make this clear, but allude to the idea). In the end, most of the contestants, especially the women, walk away hurt and wounded. Sometimes, after all this intimacy, the bachelor rejects the last person standing. The other option is a marriage proposal, and at times, he proposes only to reject her a few weeks later! Here she is, after having "outlasted" all the others, only to be told she is not wanted. What a cycle of hurt and rejection.

If you spend a lot of time alone with someone and become intimate with that person, a significant and intimate bond develops. You are bonded together by sharing different forms of intimacy that should be reserved for marriage. If you develop these deep soul connections with people you don't intend to marry, when you eventually separate, it is tearing apart something that has been glued together. Furthermore, if you are sexually involved, you will experience even more hurt and disappointment because you have become "one flesh."

> For this reason a man will leave his father and mother and be united to his wife, and they will become one flesh". (Genesis 2:24 NIV)

Courting, on the other hand, is a relationship where the goal is to find out whether or not you are compatible for marriage. It is often done with a sense that this could be the right person. It may sound old fashioned, but it will save you much heartache and pain. Unlike dating, courting has a purpose. It's not trying out people until you find the right one. It starts with the assumption that this is someone you could potentially marry.

So You Are Interested in Someone?

Here are some steps to take if you are honestly interested in someone and you believe there may be potential for marriage.

1. Ask God. Have you asked God what He thinks? It seems so easy, but how often do we ask God first? "In all your ways know, recognize, and acknowledge Him, and He will direct and make straight and plain your paths" (Prov. 3:6 AMP).

2. Spend time in group settings rather than alone. Once you get to a point where you are ready to go to the next level, be "alone in a crowd." Go to a restaurant or place where you can talk without the pressure of physical intimacy.

3. Ask spiritually sound friends, mentors, and family members. See what they think of the person. There is safety in a multitude of counselors (see Prov. 11:14).

4. Don't rush things. You can find out a lot more about a person in the context of a friendship than you can once things get physical. Once it turns physical, the physical relationship becomes your focus.

5. Is the person willing to wait if you are unsure? If there is pressure to advance too quickly, this may not be the right person. Like you, they should want to go through the complete process in order to find out if it's the Lord's will to proceed.

Friendship Relationships

Friendships can have a huge impact on our walk of faith. I once heard a preacher say, "When God wants to bless you, He brings a person into your life. When the enemy wants to curse you, he brings a person into your life." Your friendships can make or break you. Let me explain.

Proverbs 13:20 says, "He who walks with the wise grows wise, but a companion of fools suffers harm" (NIV). This verse is self-explanatory. Walk with wise and godly people, and you will become wise. Hang out with fools, and you will be a fool! 1 Corinthians 15:33 says, "Don't be fooled by those who say such things, for 'bad company corrupts good character.'" People who say evil and corrupt things and those who do not tell the truth will corrupt you. Be very careful who you choose as friends, especially in college. Your faith is vulnerable enough because of your stage of life and the transition you have just undergone. The environment you find yourself in is one that often seeks to undermine faith rather than encourage it. Trust me, you are going to need people who build up your faith!

It's not that you shouldn't be friends with people who are different from you, including people of different faith backgrounds. How else will they see Christ? Your life can be enriched through these relationships as well. I'm simply saying, *don't yoke yourself to someone who is not on the same page.* Seek out a good church and campus fellowship right away and find some friends who are following Christ with everything they have! Deliberately surround yourself with people who are more on fire for Jesus than you are.

Some relationships are only for a season. It's a hard thing to do, but sometimes you have to note that and move on. It could be that you are investing way more into the relationship than the other person. It could be that you have outgrown that person, who no longer wants to go where you are going. It's not about being cut-throat. It's simply a reality that you outgrow some friendships. One of the hardest things in life is to recognize that and move on. Many times friendships can drift apart because you are both moving in different directions.

In Proverbs 27:17 it says, "As iron sharpens iron, so one man sharpens another" (NIV). A true friend sharpens, challenges, and makes you a better person. True friends are not afraid to help you see a blind spot in your life. You need people like this. Don't just surround yourself with "yes men"—those who will only tell you only what you want to hear. True friends may be the source of some friction. The things they sometimes tell you can sting, but in the end, they will make you a better person and a more devoted follower of Jesus!

The Bible says, "Open rebuke is better than love carefully concealed. Faithful are the wounds of a friend, but the kisses of an enemy are deceitful" (Prov. 27:5-6). A friend who loves is a friend who will tell you the truth. If you see someone you love headed toward danger and you don't tell them, is that really love? Love lives for the good of others and requires time, openness, risk, and transparency.

My wife had a friend in Bible School like this. Gina was living her life for herself—smoking, sneaking out on weekends, coming back after curfew, and making bad relationship choices (all normal on a secular college campus, but in Bible School, it's a big deal). One of her friends came to her room one night and confronted her about it. Gina remembers it very vividly and still talks about it to this day. *This young lady helped Gina turn a corner.* Similarly, I've had other pastors and mentors take me to task about things I was doing that were going to hurt me if not dealt with. It stung at the time, but I'm so thankful I didn't get offended and run away. It blessed my life and made me grow. Who knows where I would be today if I had decided not to listen?

"Some friends don't help, but a true friend is closer than your own family" (Proverbs 18:24 CEV). Real friends can even be closer than your family. In fact, they are family. You are not going to have a lot of these people in your life, so when you find one, hold onto him or her!

Hopefully this has given you an accurate picture of the importance of choosing the right relationships. It's not meant to be comprehensive, but only a general guide on the subject. For additional reading, see the list at the end of the chapter.

Discussion Questions

1. Are you in a "dating" relationship? Examine this person in light of the "Qualities to Look for in a Mate" and the "So You Are Interested in Someone" sections.
2. What did you find out?
3. What is your understanding of dating vs. courting?
4. Are you involved in inappropriate physical intimacy with anyone? What are you going to do about it?
5. Do you have any close friends who love you enough to tell you the truth? Ask them what they really think about you and your life right now? Are you are willing to hear them without being offended?

Resources

I Kiss Dating Goodbye by Joshua Harris
The Power and Purpose of Singleness by Mike Cavanaugh

Meditation Verse

Do not be unequally yoked together with unbelievers. For what fellowship has righteousness with lawlessness? And what communion has light with darkness? (2 Corinthians 6:14)

PART 5

PRACTICAL WISDOM FOR STUDENTS

Part of becoming a mature follower of Jesus is applying practical wisdom. In this section you will learn the keys to making good decisions, defending your faith, and properly managing money.

CHAPTER 11

MAKING GOOD DECISIONS

Good decision-making is one of the most important skills in life, and trust me, you will need good decision-making skills through these crucial transition years. Some of the decisions you make during this time will set the tone for the next twenty years. A seemingly small adjustment in these years can keep you on course or steer you off course ten, fifteen, or twenty years down the road. In flying or boating, steering off course even a little bit drastically affects how close you come to your final destination.

When I was young, I did not make good decisions. I reaped the fruit of many of those bad decisions, and many of them were redeemed by God's grace when He wiped the slate clean in my life. Only by God's grace am I alive, not addicted to anything, without a baby out of wedlock, and without a sexually transmitted disease. There are consequences or rewards to every choice. We must think about more than ourselves when making important decisions. Who will it affect? How will it affect them? How will this choice affect me, my friends and family, and my future spouse and children? How will it affect my life in twenty years?

Motive

Our motives are very important in the decision-making process. Our primary motive should be to glorify God–acknowledging His greatness and giving Him honor and worship in everything we do.

> Everyone who is called by My name, Whom I have created for My glory; I have formed him, yes, I have made him. (Isaiah 43:7)

First and foremost in God's economy is His glory. At first glance, that may seem conceited or self-centered, but then again, He is the only one who calls Himself, "I AM." The best thing a loving God could do for humanity is to shift our focus to the One who is worthy and deserving of it.

> Not to us, O LORD, not to us, but to your name give glory, for the sake of your steadfast love and your faithfulness! (Psalm 115:1)

Without even trying, we are "me" focused. He is the only one worthy of our whole hearts, our allegiance, and our worship. It really is all about Him, and the primary question we should be asking is when making a decision is, "Is this for God's glory or mine?" This question is a good starting point for any decision.

Living by love will always glorify God. I once heard *love* defined as "living for the good of others." I like that definition more than most others I have heard. It gives us a bottom line, and I like bottom lines. It's simple and direct. If we live our lives according to love (how will my decision affect others), we will make good decisions. Many times our decisions are "me"-centered instead of God-centered and others-centered.

Consequences and Rewards

We can't talk about decision-making without talking about consequences. *What will the consequences of my choice be?* Thinking about consequences can hinder us from making bad choices and propel us into making good choices. It seems as if teenagers and college students especially have a hard time making decisions in light of consequences. Here are some examples of questions we should ask ourselves in the decision-making process:

Is this decision going to bring me closer to God or move me farther away from Him?
Is it going to bring me closer to His plan or steer me farther away from Him?
Will this hurt someone in my life?
Am I only considering myself in this?
What is my motive?

Wise Counsel

Where there is no guidance the people fall, but in abundance of counselors there is victory. (Proverbs 11:14 NASB)

Without consultation, plans are frustrated, but with many counselors they succeed. (Proverbs 15:22 NASB)

Proverbs is called the book of wisdom, and it gives us many keys to living a successful life in God. Obtaining wise counsel is an important part of making good decisions. This is especially true when it comes to life-changing decisions like where to go to college or whether or not you should go to college. Life-changing decisions should never be made until we have sought wise counsel. Those who don't want to seek out wise counsel are foolish. Even the world understands this. That's why the

President of the United States has a cabinet and advisors. If seeking wise counsel is so important, what hinders us from doing it? Could it be that our pride can't handle someone saying, "That's a bad idea" or "You are way off-base here?" God wants us to seek wise counsel as a protection, not a hindrance. He is more interested in our success than we are! There are people older and wiser than us who have walked through the very things we are walking through, and God has ordained them to help us. These are people who love and care about us, who want to see us succeed, and they may see something we aren't seeing.

If every important person in your life is giving you similar counsel, you would do well to listen. God is probably trying to tell you something. One of the people I always take very seriously in the decision-making process is my wife. God has placed her in my life for many reasons, one of those being to help me where I am weak. She sees things differently than I do and usually has a keen decision-making sense. I know that if she is not comfortable with a direction I am proposing, I would be wise to heed her advice—so much so that I usually will not move forward until we are in agreement.

For example, before we made the decision to move to Rochester, NY to work with the main office of BASIC College Ministries, we were thinking about doing their campus missionary program. This allows people to raise their missionary support, funnel it through BASIC, and work as a missionary and campus pastor to the campus in their community while still working under the leadership of their local church. Sounds great, right? Well, it is a great program, but it wasn't what God had for us at that time. I was gung-ho about it. I knew there was some connection to BASIC that God wanted us to have, and I was right about that. But my wife just didn't feel at peace about that step. I was a little frustrated about this, but recognized by this time that there was probably a reason for her unrest. Six months later, we had the opportunity to move to Rochester, NY, and begin working with BASIC Main to work toward becoming the director of the whole ministry! As my wife and I prayed about this, we both had a sense of peace from the Lord. Although it was a much larger decision and involved moving our whole family, we both knew it was right. I tend to be a visionary and see things far off. But with that gift also comes a tendency to jump the gun, so I have learned to just take a step back and seek wise counsel before moving ahead.

Early on in my Christian walk, I wasn't so good at this. I knew I was called by God to be in vocational ministry. At the time, I was helping with the youth ministry in my church. Somehow I thought it was the time to step out and enter full time ministry, even though I didn't have any opportunities to do so. In my zeal for the Lord, I had seen the call correctly, but my sense of timing was way off! My pastor at the time wisely told me it was not the time and that I should continue to work my job and faithfully volunteer and that one day the right opportunity would arise. Had I stepped out at that time, I'm not sure what type of mess I would have gotten myself into.

Maybe you don't have a wife or husband yet, but I'm sure there are some people in your life you can seek wise counsel from— your parents, a grandmother, aunt or uncle, a friend who is walking closely with the Lord, your pastor, an older married couple, and so forth.

A pastor friend of mine taught me four things to consider when approaching an important decision:

1. What does your spouse say?
2. What do the leaders or spiritual authorities in your life say (that includes your parents)?
3. What does your "inner witness" tell you (In other words, do you have a sense that God is speaking and leading)?
4. What do the natural circumstances tell you (are they aligning with what you feel God is saying)?[1]

If you are single, what do your parents think about the decision you are making? Even if your parents are not believers, you should still honor them by hearing them out. Remember, the fifth commandment, "Honor your father and mother, that your days may be long in the land that the Lord your God is giving you" (Exodus 20:12). Honor means "to make weighty, prevail, or to make glorious."[5] Maybe you don't have a mother or father, and your grandmother, grandfather, aunt, uncle, or someone else raised you. The principle still applies. The question is, *who has parental authority in your life?* God can speak through your parents or parental authorities whether they are saved or not. That is how much He honors parental authority!

If you know very clearly that God has spoken to you, and have received council from trusted friends and other authorities in your life but your parents don't agree with your decision, what's next? There is a godly way to disagree with your parents and still honor them:

1. Hear them out in full.
2. Give weight to their words, consider what they are saying, and promise to think and pray about it. There may be pieces of counsel the Lord is speaking to you through them.
3. If you need to disagree, disagree with them in a godly way— with honor and respect rather than anger and contempt.
4. Let them know you love them and appreciate their care and concern for you.

The Word of God

It is very important, when making major decisions, to hear from the Lord. Many times this will happen through a verse from the Bible that you know He is speaking to your situation. Sometimes He will speak to your heart very clearly and directly. Other times it may come over time. However He does it, it will ultimately line up with the written Word of God and will never go against it.

During our first year with BASIC, we had a lot of difficulty raising our financial support. We knew God had called us to BASIC, but we didn't realize how hard it would be. We went into it with no training or experience. After nearly a year, when some major donors decreased their support (they had agreed to a hefty sum that would taper-off over time), we were struggling badly. Gina and I got on our faces like we had in the past when we were having financial struggles and began asking God to show us whether I should look for part-time work. The Lord showed us very clearly through a Scripture that we were not to do this. We were to trust Him instead:

> Now to Him who is able to do far more abundantly beyond all that we ask or think, according to the power that works within us. (Ephesians 3:20 NASB)

Upon reading it and hearing it, we knew the Lord was speaking to us. Peace came over our hearts, and our minds were made up. It doesn't always happen this way, but many times the Lord will confirm important decisions through the written Word of God. Then, when we do experience the hardship that inevitably comes with following Christ we have an anchor to hold us steady. We know beyond a shadow of a doubt that God has led us and directed us. When we don't have this surety, it's easy to back out when things get tough.

Here's another way to look at it. As we view things in light of God's written Word, it can often make decisions more clear. There are times when we are immediately able to rule an option out based on whether or not a biblical principle applies. Let me give you an example. We are now in the iPod age. We can download songs and movies, burn CD's, and rip tracks from CD's to put on our iPods. If we want to, we can steal music without paying for it. Sometimes, we want share these songs with others or burn a CD for a friend. The truth is it is against the law to do this (unless, of course, they are offered legally). Romans 13 tells us that we are to submit to the governing authorities, and the governing authorities have made an anti-piracy law. Every time we download music illegally, we are actually stealing from the artist. So, regardless of how we feel about doing this, and regardless of whether or not "everyone is doing it," it's illegal. As Christians, we should refrain from doing this in accordance with Romans 13. This is what I mean when I say God's Word can guide us in making right decisions. When we know and understand God's Word, we can rule out certain options immediately based on what it says.

Peace in Decision Making

God's peace is supernatural and with it comes the ability to guard our hearts and minds. It brings prosperity, quietness, and rest to our souls. It's an anchor we can rely on in the most difficult of storms. Jesus Himself is our peace (see Ephesians 2:14).

> Don't worry about anything; instead, pray about everything. Tell God what you need, and thank Him for all He has done. Then you will experience God's peace, which exceeds anything we can understand. His peace will guard your hearts and minds as you live in Christ Jesus. (Philippians 4:6-7 NLT)

My wife and I have never lacked for God's peace when making major life-changing decisions. That's not to say we haven't struggled over decisions or had times where we felt unsure. In smaller decisions, when we don't have a clear sense of guidance about a decision and we have applied some of the guiding principles I've talked about already, we just figure God really trusts us! After all, we are not robots or clones. Remember, God isn't trying to hide His will from us. He wants us to succeed more than we want to succeed! If we are diligent to seek God, we will find Him (see Proverbs 8:17). One way we discern His will is by looking for His peace. Do we have peace in our hearts and minds in the situation–supernatural peace that surpasses understanding? When I find His peace, it gives me confidence to actually make a decision.

Research

When making major decisions, we should research all our options, unless, of course, we've heard very clearly from Jesus; in which case, obedience, not research, is the proper action. It's often through research that we learn what God does *not* want or what does *not* appeal to us, thereby eliminating certain options. If we research something fully and it is still not completely clear to us, at least we can make an informed decision.

The Peak-to-Peak Principle

This is a simple principle, but it goes a long way. We should make major decisions when we are at the top of the peak, not in the valley.

> When we're in the valleys of life, we don't see clearly. Our perspective is limited, and all we see are the problems around us. *In the valleys we make decisions, not to better ourselves, but to escape our problems.* Never make a major decision in the valleys. Wait until you get to the peak where you can see clearer and farther. By reserving big choices for the peaks, you'll avoid making rash decisions that you'll regret later (emphasis added).[3]

One of my pastors said it this way "The valley is for changing you. The mountain top is for changing direction." He would explain that when we are at the top, we have a better view; we can make decisions based on clear sight, success, and a happier state of life. Decisions tend to be better when we are in that frame of mind. When we are in the valley, it is difficult; we can't see very far because everything is in a shadow.[4] Here is one example from this pastor's life. After pastoring successfully for twenty years, he decided it was time to relinquish his role, feeling like he was on the peak. Rather than wait another ten years, until things were declining or until he had stayed too long, he felt like he had the most insight and clarity at that moment. As a result, he sought to transition the church then, at the peak, instead of waiting five or ten years when he or the church may have been in the valley.

Minor Decisions

So far, we have spoken a lot about major decisions, but what about the small ones? During major decisions, it seems as if God's leading is often very clear, albeit difficult to step out in faith. But minor decisions can sometimes be difficult to make when we do not have a clear direction from the Lord. *It's the little decisions that can paralyze us.* In those times, we must follow the principles of God's Word, research the facts, and make the best decision possible. It's important not to become paralyzed with indecision. There are times when it's necessary to make a well-informed decision rather than no decision. Indecision hinders forward momentum. Even if we take a wrong turn in the integrity of our hearts to do right, it doesn't mean we have to go back to square one. No one makes it through life without taking a wrong turn. If we make a mistake (mistakes done with a heart to do the right thing), we learn from it, grow, and move on. I have learned many important life-lessons by making mistakes. It doesn't mean we are failures; it means we are learners, and it qualifies us to help others *through our mistakes.*

Choosing a College

When making a decision about when and where to go to college, one of the first questions you should ask, *Is God calling me to go to college, and am I ready for college?* Why are you going to college? Is it to get out of the house? Tired of your parents? You want your freedom, or you want to party? But is God *calling* you to go to college? Walt Henrichsen, the author of *Disciples Are Made Not Born*, made this statement: "If you are going to college for any other reason than to be a missionary for Jesus Christ, you are there for selfish, sinful reasons."[5] In the same way, God wants us to find our passion and use it to bring glory to Him. Whatever our profession, this is simply a vehicle to carry out His calling in our lives and reach the people around us for Christ. In His book *The Fuel and the Flame,* Steve Shadrach uses this line of questioning to discover motive:

Question: "So why did you come to college?"

Response: "I'm here to get a good education."

Question: "Okay... but why do you want a good education?"

Response: "Well... because I want to get a good job."

Question: "A good job, huh? Why is it you want to get a good job?"

Response: "Okay, I admit it. I want a good job so I can get a better salary."

Question: "Well, why would you want a better salary?"

Response (after some prodding): "So that we can support the kind of comfortable lifestyle we have dreamed about."[6]

Our motive many times is not to glorify God, but to live the American dream: go to college, get a good job, have a comfortable life with 1.5 kids, buy a house in the suburbs with a white picket fence, retire to Florida and play golf every day until the Lord takes me home. It's all centered around our personal comfort. If we are followers of Jesus, our motive must be to advance God's kingdom for God's glory. This comes out of having an intimate relationship with Him. Then your motive will probably look more like this: "God is calling me to go to college to be a missionary to those around me and to study in order to prepare myself to advance His kingdom on the earth."

Some young people aren't ready for college as soon as they graduate from high school. Others may be ready for college, but are not ready to leave home. Is it possible that you might consider taking a year to build your character and solidify your relationship with God? There are lots of opportunities, like doing missions work, going to Bible School for a year, or doing an internship at your church or another non-profit. Why not take a year to do something that doesn't advance your agenda but God's? Maybe you should consider going to community college for a year or two while serving God in your local church (you might save yourself a lot of debt as well). A year or two can make a big difference in maturity. Many people who come right out of high school are just not ready for the challenges that college will bring. They lack the maturity and responsibility to handle that level of freedom. I'm not saying you shouldn't go to college, but just that you need to use wisdom in your approach.

You may not believe me, but the statistics don't lie. As I

shared with you in Chapter 1, "Most experts believe 70% of college students who have grown up in church will drop out (of church) when they go to college."[7] You are not exempt. If you decide to go away to college, you need to be sure that God is calling you to go and that your faith is solid. Otherwise, you may become a statistic. This isn't a threat or a scare tactic. I am only asking you to seriously pray and consider this important decision a little more carefully. Give it the weight it deserves. It's not something to be taken lightly. Ask your parents, mentors, or some older people who know you well to seriously evaluate your level of maturity so that you have some transparent input as you make this decision. And the fact of the matter is, if you can't handle real and honest input, you are probably not mature enough to thrive in college.

College Debt

So many students get in over their heads with college debt. Most of the time (I say most of the time because I have broken my own rule on occasion), I go by the principle, *if you can't afford it, don't buy it.* I think the same applies for college. Trust me, you don't want to be paying off mounds of debt for thirty years after you graduate college. I know you want to get out of the house, away from the parents, and have independence, but there are more important things to think about. Six months after college is over, the bank comes calling, and sometimes before you even find a good job, you are paying a college loan equivalent to a house payment! My student loans are not overwhelming, but fifteen years later, I'm still paying them. If I knew then what I know now, I may have done some things differently. Here are some options to consider:

- Consider going to community college for two years. You can live at home and knock out the majority of the general classes you need at a fraction of the cost!
- Look for grants. There are plenty out there if you just spend the time looking for them. Some people take a whole summer to research grants full-time instead of working a job. In doing this, some have funded their college education!

- Go where you can afford. If you have access to a university that you can attend for a great price, do it!

God wants to direct you in your choosing of a college. He has a plan. Remember, the righteous person's steps are ordered of the Lord (see Psalms 37:23; Proverbs 16:9; 20:24). Take the time to find His plan and follow it!

Discussion Questions and Action Steps

1. What are the major decisions you are facing right now?
2. List them and go through the following steps throughout the next week:

   a. Pray—What is God saying to me?

   b. Seek wise counsel from at least two or three people.

   c. What does the Word of God say?

   d. Do I have peace from God about this decision?

   e. Will it bring God glory?

   f. Have I researched it adequately?

   g. Can I afford it?

Meditation Verses

The LORD directs the steps of the godly. He delights in every detail of their lives. (Psalms 37:23 NLT)

CHAPTER 12

DEFENDING YOUR FAITH

*Many Christians settle for simplicity on the near side of complexity. Their faith is only mind deep. They know **what** they believe, but they don't know **why** they believe what they believe. Their faith is fragile because it has never been tested intellectually or experientially. Near-side Christians have never been in the catacombs of doubt or suffering, so when they encounter questions they cannot answer or experiences they cannot explain, it causes a crisis of faith. For far-side Christians, those who have done their time in the catacombs of doubt or suffering, unanswerable questions and unexplainable experiences actually result in a heightened appreciation for the mystery and majesty of a God who does not fit within the logical constraints of the left brain. Near-side Christians, on the other hand, lose their faith before they've really found it.[1] - Mark Batterson*

But in your hearts honor Christ the Lord as holy, always being prepared to make a defense to anyone who asks you for a reason for the hope that is in you; yet do it with gentleness and respect, having a good conscience, so that, when you are slandered, those who revile your good behavior in Christ may be put to shame. (1 Peter 3:15-16 ESV)

With the bombardment of all the ism's—humanism, intellectualism, secularism, and post-modernism—you had better be strong in your faith and convictions and be ready to defend them vigorously! At some colleges and universities, I've heard there are certain professors whose goal is actually to derail the faith of Christians. Even if they do out-think you and you don't know all the answers or don't have a defense for every argument, make up your mind before you get there that you will follow Jesus regardless of the cost! College is a normal period in life to question things. It is a time for your faith to become real. You are going to have doubts. You are not going to have all the answers. Questions are OK. It's what you do with those questions that matters. Don't just rely on your skeptical professors or classmates for answers; take your questions to mature Christians who can help you sort through them.

This is where relationship also comes in. Your relationship with Jesus must be strong. Use it as a time to delve deeper. Throughout many intense transitions in life, the only thing that kept me was a strong abiding relationship with Jesus. When doubt and uncertainty swirled around me, it was looking into the steady eyes of Jesus that carried me through.

There are times when your faith is fragile and you need to keep yourself away from books or even relationships that may cause you to question your faith, especially if you are a new believer. Get around mature followers of Christ, find a Bible-believing church, make sure you attend a Christian fellowship on campus, and continue to feed your mind with the Word of God and Christian literature. I'm not saying insulate or isolate yourself against everything around you that's not Christian. I'm simply saying be selective about the influences you allow into your life during uncertain times.

During college, I got into reading some philosophical fiction books. My senior year, still very new in my faith, I started to read a book by Ayn Rand called, *Atlas Shrugged*. About fifty pages into it, God spoke to my heart very clearly: "Do not read this book." I was not accustomed to hearing the voice of God at that point and shrugged it off as some odd anomaly. I continued to read the book, and by the end of it, my faith was in question—so much so that I wasn't sure if I believed Christianity anymore or that my experience with Jesus was real. I was in a full-fledged faith crisis, so I went back to the place where it all began, the chapel on my campus. I cried out to God, asking for His help, asking Him to show me that He was real.

When I did that, something profound happened. The presence of God came over me, and I actually began to speak in a language I didn't understand. I even thought I knew what I was praying! What came to my mind was, "Guide me, my Captain. Guide me, my Captain." Whatever I was saying (as I said, I didn't know or understand the language), this supernatural experience instantly wiped away all my doubt and unbelief. I was suddenly at peace and didn't fret over whether or not God was real any longer! Maybe you think that's weird, but it totally put my mind and heart at rest. It was supernatural and unexplainable. It's exactly what I needed at the time. Divine encounters can shape us and change our trajectory.

It's important that you experience God's presence profoundly *and* that you renew your mind. In college, your faith will be bombarded and tested. Your intellect will have to be sharp and your trust in God solidly founded in a close personal relationship and in the Word of God. People shouldn't be able to sway your faith with intellectual arguments. If someone brings up an argument you can't handle or don't have an answer for, ask someone more experienced, find a good Christian book that addresses it, or if need be, back away from the relationship if this person is making you continually question your faith. It's not bad to have questions and doubts about things. If handled properly, this can actually strengthen your faith, but if something or someone is undermining your faith, you may need to take a step back until you are mature enough to handle it.

After being a follower of Jesus for over fifteen years, I still have many unanswered questions, but I don't let it sway my faith. My relationship with God is real and life-giving. God has been good to me, and His presence is very real to me, so when I don't understand things or when I have questions, I research, talk to people and I take them to God, and whether I get an answer or not, it doesn't cause my faith to be swayed. Many times, I don't get an answer to my question, but I get Him – and all that comes with Him: peace, love, joy, fulfillment, hope, strength, and love, to name a few.

The Mind

The enemy's main point of attack is our mind. We must learn to take thoughts captive and combat lies with truth:

> For though we walk (live) in the flesh, we are not carrying on our warfare according to the flesh and using mere human weapons. For the weapons of our warfare are not physical [weapons of flesh and blood], but they are mighty before God for the overthrow and destruction of strongholds (a castle or fortress), [Inasmuch as we] *refute arguments and theories and reasoning's* and every proud and lofty thing that sets itself up against the [true] knowledge of God; and *we lead every thought and purpose away captive into the obedience of Christ* (the Messiah, the Anointed One) (Emphasis mine). (2 Corinthians 10:35 AMP)

Our weapon is the Word of God, the Bible, the truth. It is our sword (see Eph. 6:17). We must throw down arguments and theories that contend with God's Word. I don't mean fight against people who are arguing with us (we don't war according to the flesh). I mean – we use the Word of God to cast down and cut down arguments that would undermine our faith, just as Jesus did as He was tempted by Satan in the wilderness. Each time Satan tried to tell Him a half truth, Jesus used the Word of God to hurl it down (see Luke 4:1-12). We can learn a lot from Jesus' example. I suggest going back and reading it.

You must make a decision that, no matter how good the argument or how much you don't understand about God, you are going to continue trusting Him. Jesus is not just an intellectual concept; He is a person with whom you have a relationship. It's relating to Him, by knowing His Word and by experiencing His presence and His love that gets you through things you don't understand. He's God. He's infinite. He's huge. How could we possibly understand everything about Him as small, limited, finite beings? I once heard pastor Bill Johnson of Bethel Church say, "If I understand all that is going on in my Christian life, I have an inferior Christian life."

Transformation

One of the primary ways to defend your faith against the arguments, theories, intellectualism (the view that regards the intellect as superior to the will and has a high regard for intellectual pursuits[2]), and vain and hollow philosophies is to renew your mind. Part of being able to defend your faith is learning how to keep your faith in the wake of criticism, contempt, and persecution. In order to do that, you must have a renewed mind. An un-renewed mind will hinder you from growing and being transformed in your Christian walk. It's hard work, and it takes persistence, but it's worth it!

A couple years ago, I was preaching on transformation while at the same time asking God to transform me as well. During that season, I wanted to do some work on my lower driveway that was all gravel. I needed a heavy-duty steel rake but didn't have one. One day, while surveying the job, I saw a rake, just like the one I needed, lying near some large stones in my front yard. The previous owners had left it behind. I was very excited that I didn't have to buy a new rake. In that moment, the Lord spoke something I will never forget about renewing the mind. He said, "I have given you all the tools you need, but I'm not going to rake the lawn for you."

My perspective immediately shifted. I realized that it was my responsibility to renew and renovate my mind. Renovation is no easy process; it takes time and hard work. Everything we need has been provided for in Christ (see 2 Peter 1:3), but that doesn't mean we don't have to exert any effort. We don't work to secure the gift of salvation; that has already been done. But we do have to exert grace-filled effort to implement what God has already provided. God isn't going to memorize Scripture for us and apply it to our lives; that's our responsibility. He doesn't leave us to do it on our own either–His grace and power are always available through the Holy Spirit to help us.

Renewing Our Minds

> Therefore, I urge you, brothers, in view of God's mercy, to offer your bodies as living sacrifices, holy and pleasing to God—this is your spiritual act of worship. Do not conform any longer to the pattern of this world, but be transformed by the renewing of your mind. Then you will be able to test and approve what God's will is—his good, pleasing and perfect will. (Romans 12:1-2 NIV)

According to this passage, we must first offer ourselves *entirely* to God. It's called lordship. Jesus doesn't just want part of us; He wants *all* of us. He didn't die to pay part of the price. He died to pay the *whole* price. He gave everything for us, and we must give everything for Him. It's all for all. This is our reasonable act of worship.

Additionally, we must not be conformed, pushed, or molded into the same pattern as the world. The world has patterns of thinking and acting that are contrary to the ways of God. The university system wants to mold your minds into its pattern, but the way we think should be molded by God's thoughts and ways (see Isaiah 55:8-9), not by vain arguments and hollow philosophies. We have the truth that the world so desperately needs and we must not trade it in for something lesser, something perishable, or something inferior.

Finally, we are to be transformed by the renewing of our minds. The word *transformed* is from the Greek word *metamorphoo*.[3] It means "to change, transfigure, or transform."

Transformation—trans'fer ma' shen—To change in form, appearance, or structure, metamorphose. To change in condition, nature, character; convert. *To change into another substance* (italics mine).

What an awesome truth. As we renew our minds by the Word of God and begin to think like Him, we are changed into new people! Obviously, one of the best pictures we have of metamorphosis is that of a butterfly. They change from an egg, to larva (caterpillar), to a pupa (resting stage), to a beautiful adult butterfly. Like the butterfly, we too can actually change forms by the renewing of our minds.

The word *renew* actually means "to renovate." Dictionary.com defines renovate as:

> **Renovate**—To restore to good condition, as by repairing or remodeling. To reinvigorate, refresh. *Make as something new* (italics mine).

Renovation is hard work, and God's not going to do it for us. He has provided and will provide, in an ongoing way, the grace and power to do it, but He will not do it for us. Old things have to be demolished or stripped down. Then we have to start fresh by restoring, replacing, rebuilding, or renewing with the right ways of thinking found in the Word of God.

Maybe you've seen the popular television show, *Extreme Makeover—Home Edition*. When the show started, they didn't tear down the whole house and start over as they do now. Instead, they would totally renovate and remodel the existing house. Even then, it took a large crew seven days just to renovate a single house. It's not an easy job. It requires blood, sweat, and tears. God has given us His Word as a tool and a weapon to fix problems and fight enemies, but we, with the Holy Spirits help, must do the hard work of renovation. It reminds me of Nehemiah. They built the wall with one hand and in the other hand held a sword to defend against enemy attacks.

We come into this new life in Christ with a lot of baggage and old ways of thinking. It's true that if any of us are in Christ, we are new creations (see 2 Corinthians 5:17). We are "born again" and made new (see John 3:3), but that doesn't mean all our old ways of thinking suddenly vanish. Egypt doesn't so easily leave us. When the children of Israel left slavery in Egypt to begin the journey toward the Promised Land, they complained the whole way. They complained about how hard it was, about eating only manna, about how good it had been in Egypt (keep in mind they were slaves). They complained right up until they got to the doors of the Promised Land! My point is, we often look back and lament about how hard change is and how good we thought we had it before the process of change begins, even though we were slaves to sin and the world. Those old ways of thinking aren't so easily broken. This process of renewing our minds takes Spirit-empowered work.

Here are a couple of things about to keep in mind about renovation and renewing our minds:

1. We need a plan—Identify the areas or "strongholds" that need to undergo renovation, find a Scripture to address it, and begin the hard work of renovating the way you think.

2. It's a process—It won't happen overnight, so be patient. Don't be overly hard on yourself. Enlist a partner to share this process with you. Sometimes it's hard to see the change happening in ourselves.

3. It takes work—We are going to have to get our hands dirty in the process. God has given us everything we need; let's put it to good use! Pray, meditate on the Word of God, and allow it to shape and change you!

Finally, it's by renewing and renovating our minds that we are able to know God's perfect will (see Romans 12:2)! One of the most common questions people have is, "How do I find God's will?" Wow! Apparently the way we do that is by renewing our minds with His Word. His Word is His will. When we have, see, and comprehend revelation, we know His will.

As we surrender all, reject the pattern of this world, and are transformed by the renewing of our minds, we discover His good, pleasing, and perfect will.

Be Persistent

If you are a Christian in college, you will be bombarded by attitudes, philosophies, and beliefs that will be radically different from those in the Bible. If you are outspoken, you may even be belittled and mildly persecuted by your peers and professors. I say *mildly* because in comparison to what others around the world face for believing in Jesus, it is mild. Be encouraged; it's all worth it! Begin to think from a heavenly perspective and get educated on some of the questions and criticisms you will face. Learn how to defend your faith in a biblical way. And remember, if you are ridiculed, you are in good company:

> Blessed are those who have been persecuted for the sake of righteousness, for theirs is the kingdom of heaven. Blessed are you when **people** insult you and persecute you, and falsely say all kinds of evil against you because of Me. Rejoice and be glad, for your reward in heaven is great; for in the same way they persecuted the prophets who were before you. (Matthew 4:10-12 NASB)

I remember being a baby Christian my junior year of college. One day I had a shirt on with a Scripture on the back. One of my geology professors began to question me on it in front of the whole class. His closing statement (said rather sarcastically) was, "OK, if that works for you..." Although he didn't harp on it for too long, he did point me out in front of the whole class and question my young faith. I could have let it destroy my faith. After all, he was a tenured professor. But my relationship with Jesus was real and life-giving. It's OK if you don't have all the answers. Defend your faith anyway. Nothing in this life compares to what you are going to find in the next. It's a good time for training. There will be questions and arguments you can't answer, but ask, seek, knock, read, and study, and you will find the answers. Only you know the relationship you have with your Savior; don't let anything or anyone persuade you otherwise. During this stage of life, it is normal to have questions about your faith. No question is too big for God. Talk to God, read, and talk to others who have walked through questions like these. God is not repulsed by an inquisitive nature. You are His child; He welcomes your questions, but you must come to the point where you say, "Even if I don't understand something about God or life, I'm going to trust Him."

People and institutions are not our enemies. Jesus came to seek and save those who are lost (see Luke 19:10). Our enemy is Satan and his demons, who are holding people hostage in darkness and bondage. As the apostle Paul wrote, "We are not fighting against humans. We are fighting against forces and authorities and against rulers of darkness and powers in the spiritual world" (Eph. 6:12 CEV). Our minds must be transformed to God's way of thinking. Like Jesus, we must say, "Father forgive them for they know not what they do" (Luke 23:34).

You are a shining ray of light in your high school, on your campus, and in your job! Often the people who criticize you the most are also the most open. If you stand strong in His grace and live your life as an example, you will have an impact on those around you.

I can't tell you all the areas where you should sharpen your faith, but I can tell you a few of the issues that you may be questioned or confronted about: evolution, sexuality, religious pluralism (there are many ways to God), intellectualism, rationalism (knowledge derives mostly from reason and reasoning), and secular humanism (rejects the supernatural and religion as the basis of morality). There are biblical answers for all of these things and good books on each subject. I have listed a few resources at the end of the chapter. Whether you know all the answers or not, you should be ready to defend your faith scripturally and share your testimony with anyone who asks!

It's also very important to be in community with other believers on campus and a local church. College is a place where you need a support network. Statistics show that a very high percentage of Christian students either lose their faith or walk away from the Church during their first year of college. I believe one of the main reasons for this is neglecting to get involved in

Christian community. God didn't create us to live out our faith alone. There is strength in partnership. It is impossible to be connected to Christ but be separate from His body.

Daniels and Josephs

I believe God wants companies of Josephs and Daniels in our universities. Such people are willing to pay the price to see God glorified on their campus. These Josephs and Daniels have an excellent spirit in them and are empowered and endued with supernatural wisdom and creativity to solve the world's problems. By the favor of God, they have developed integrity and character that is able to withstand significant leadership challenges:

> Then this Daniel became distinguished above all the other presidents and satraps, because an excellent spirit was in him. And the king planned to set him over the whole kingdom. (Daniel 6:3 ESV)

Because of the favor of God on his life and his integrity and heart to serve God and not defile himself in this alien culture, the Lord gave Daniel an excellent spirit, causing him to stand out above the rest. We all want to be more than mediocre, but what really sets us apart is an excellent spirit given by God! Daniel never compromised his values throughout his whole time in Babylon. Time and time again, he was promoted by different kings due to the wisdom and favor God had bestowed on His life. Daniel kept his faith in the midst of a hostile culture. He excelled in his relationship with God. Even in the midst of persecution, he continued to seek God in relationship three times per day (see Daniel 6:10). God also gave him a supernatural ability to interpret dreams and visions. Like Joseph, this was a key to his promotion. When no one else could come up with an answer, Joseph and Daniel were called upon.

What if, because of your desire to follow Christ and your commitment not to compromise, God granted you an excellent spirit? What if He caused you to jut out above the rest? What if He gave you the ability to interpret the dreams and visions of professors, administrators, and university presidents? How about interpreting dreams for kings and presidents of nations? God wants to train and release whole companies of Daniels and Josephs in this hour! Maybe you are one of them.

It's important to recognize that Daniel had to make a conscious choice not to defile himself in the Babylonian culture:

> **But Daniel was determined not to defile himself by eating the food and wine given to them by the king. He asked the chief of staff for permission not to eat these unacceptable foods. (Daniel 1:8 NLT)**

Author Mark Batterson calls it a "Holy Resolution.":

> **It was a physical and spiritual resolution. And Daniel would have never** *attained his position of influence* **without making that resolution. He would have never** *interpreted dreams* **or** *become famous for surviving the lion's den* **without making that resolution.** *That single resolution changed his life!* **And his life isn't unlike ours. I know many people dismiss resolutions as short-lived ideals, but they are more than that. If they are** *promises to God* **or** *pursued for God's purposes,* **they have the power to** *alter your destiny.*[6]

Daniel and Joseph had a fragrance to their lives that went beyond the intellectual discussion and defense of their faith. They had the power of a living God to back them up! They had supernatural intellectual capacity, and they were also committed to living God's way without defiling themselves in a foreign culture. They were men of integrity and character.

I think there is a numbing effect when we engage and indulge in too much culture. *After all, we are not of this world.* When we don't limit ourselves and instead over-indulge in food, entertainment, and everything this world has to offer, we become just like the world. That's why fasting or denying ourselves is so important. In a world that indulges in every type of pleasure, we can intentionally deny our flesh, set ourselves apart for God, and let His voice and His power rise up in our hearts.

Words are often simply not enough. The pursuit of intellectual thought alone cannot change a life. What if God granted you the ability to use your intellect to find cures for cancer and AIDS? What if He gave you solutions to the world's water and food problems? What if He showed you inventions that would change the world? What if He promoted you to positions of incredible influence because of His abundant favor on your life and the integrity he had worked in your heart? It's all in God's heart, and He wants to give it. In fact, He longs to give it to those who ask and are surrendered to Him! Talk isn't enough; we need power. The greatest intellect can be awed by the supernatural. As Paul wrote in Corinthians:

My message and my preaching were not in persuasive words of wisdom, but in demonstration of the Spirit and of power, so that your faith would not rest on the wisdom of men, but on the power of God. (2 Cor. 2:4-5 NASB)

After a while, talk needs to cease and the demonstration of the Spirit and the power of God must take over. People grow tired of all talk and no action.

So pursue your intellectual studies and seek to understand and be able to articulate the gospel in an clear and succinct way, but always remember, the power is in the message itself (see Romans 1:16). Let the power of God come through you in both a natural and supernatural way and people will see that He really does exist! It will be uncomfortable at times. You will have to wade into deep water, but it's worth it!

Discussion Questions

1. Have you had any experiences where teachers, professors, or those in authority belittled you because of your faith? If so, were you ready to give a defense? What was your response?
2. Read Luke 4:1-12 afresh and discuss what you have learned from Jesus' example.
3. Have you made the decision that no matter what the cost, no matter how much persecution you receive, and no matter how many things you don't understand about God, you are going to follow Him anyway? If not, do so now!
4. In what ways of thinking do you need to be transformed by the renewing or renovating your mind? Come up with a deliberate plan and at least one Scripture for each issue that you are going to begin to memorize and apply to your life.
5. Why do you think Daniel had an excellent spirit? Are you ready to make a Holy Resolution? Maybe a first step could be to go on a 21-day Daniel Fast (no meats, sweets, or pleasing foods) to cleanse yourself from the culture and set yourself apart to God. Who knows what God could do?
6. Dream about what God could empower you to do if you had an excellent spirit. Write it down.

Resources

Appendix D: The Seven R's by Kent A. Murawski
The New Evidence That Demands a Verdict by Josh McDowell
A Ready Defense by Josh McDowell
The Blueprint by Jaeson Ma

Meditation Verse

Therefore, I urge you, brothers, in view of God's mercy, to offer your bodies as living sacrifices, holy and pleasing to God—this is your spiritual act of worship. Do not conform any longer to the pattern of this world, but be transformed by the renewing of your mind. Then you will be able to test and approve what God's will is—his good, pleasing and perfect will. (Romans 12:1-2 NIV)

CHAPTER 13

MONEY MANAGEMENT

> I am afraid the only safe rule is to give more than we can spare.—C.S. Lewis

This is one of the most important areas in all of life. I don't mean that making money is the most important thing, but *the submitting of money to the lordship of Jesus Christ and the stewardship of that money for the kingdom of God.* College is a big part of that stewardship. Many young people go to college simply so they can make more money and live the American dream. The question we need to ask ourselves is this: *Is the American dream God's dream?* Let's recall Walt Henrichson's statement, "If you are at college for any other reason than to be a missionary for Jesus Christ, you are there for selfish, sinful reasons." What then would be the right motivations for attending college?

- To be a missionary for Jesus
- To advance the kingdom of God by receiving the training for a particular field of expertise that you are gifted to do
- To advance the kingdom of God by using the money and influence that goes with receiving secondary education.
- To fulfill your God-given purpose.

I minister to Harvard students. Some of them are quite literally geniuses. There was a student who attended our church who is fairly certain he is going to major in some type of government and/or international relations. He is currently studying Arabic and sees himself influencing Middle Eastern policy. He has a natural leadership gift like few I have ever seen. I am fairly confident he is going to do many of the things he has expressed, and he will probably make a lot of money in the meantime, but he understands he is at Harvard so he can use the prestigious education he receives to influence people for the kingdom of God. There was another Harvard student named Matt who went on to study medicine at Duke. I'm fairly certain he will be one of the influencers in his field. Matt knows his gift, his intellect, and whatever influence he gains all come from God's hand, and he seeks to use his gift to help people for the glory of God.

The Debt Trap

College is where I got my first taste of debt. It was my freshman year, and outside of the dining hall is where the credit card vendors would always set up their tables. They would give away free stuff if you signed up for a credit card. Some of the stuff was cool free stuff and some was just free stuff, but it was still *free stuff* (we Americans love free stuff, don't we)! Little did I know I would get a couple credit cards in the mail several weeks later. I didn't go max them out on clothes and toys like some of my friends did, but I did use them for such things as fixing my car when I didn't have any money. Big mistake! After college, instead of saving money to start an emergency fund, I continued to use credit cards when things broke that I didn't have the money to fix or occasionally when I got in a bind.

An emergency fund is when you save three-to-six-months' worth of your normal income so that when emergencies and unexpected financial problems come (and they surely will), you have money set aside to cover it. You can start by tucking away $1,000 in a savings account and then build on it. If you are in high school, college, or simply beginning to make your way in young adulthood, you may not even have a normal income yet. I would advise that when you work your summer job or begin to have some form of an income, this is the first thing you do after tithing and paying your bills. Many refer to this concept of setting aside money as "paying yourself first." I call it paying yourself *second*, because our first and best should go to God. That means, the first thing you do after paying your tithe is to tuck away some savings. I would advise you to save 10%. If you can't do 10% right away, start with *something*. Notice, this is *not* savings for some item you would like to have. If you want to do that, start a separate savings account or wait until you have three-six months' worth of income in an emergency fund, then you can direct it toward something else. This is a fund that you *only* use in an emergency if you have no other source of income to pay for it. After using it for an emergency, immediately start to replenish it.

Jesus had a lot to say about money. Did you know 15% of all Jesus' words in the Bible were about money and resources? That is more than He talked about heaven and hell combined![87] Why did He go to such lengths? *Because He knew money would compete for the #1 place in our hearts!*

> Do not lay up for yourselves treasures on earth, where moth and rust destroy and where thieves break in and steal, but lay up for yourselves treasures in heaven, where neither moth nor rust destroys and where thieves do not break in and steal. *For where your treasure is, there your heart will be also* (Italics mine). (Matthew 6:19-21)

What is Jesus saying? *Your heart will always follow your money.* In other words, if your goal in life is to be comfortable or have lots of money, and you store it up, invest in the stock market, and have lots of stuff for your own selfish gain, you are laying up for yourself treasures on earth that *will* perish. If, on the other hand, you will honor God with your tithes and offerings, be generous and seek to put others first, you will amass a reserve of eternal treasures that can never be taken from you!

It is not wrong to take care of your needs, make money or to invest in the stock market, but first and foremost you should be honoring God with the tithe and giving regular offerings into His kingdom work. Christians are to seek first the kingdom of God and His righteousness (see Matthew 6:33). I would encourage you to read and meditate upon Matthew 6. This is a key passage in understanding money from a godly perspective.

Money Is a Test

Money is the plumb line by which God evaluates whether or not our faith is authentic and if we can be trusted with true riches.

Here's the lesson: Use your worldly resources to benefit others and make friends. Then, when your earthly possessions are gone, they will welcome you to an eternal home. If you are faithful in little things, you will be faithful in large ones. But if you are dishonest in little things, you won't be honest with greater responsibilities. *And if you are untrustworthy about worldly wealth, who will trust you with the true riches of heaven?* And if you are not faithful with other people's things, why should you be trusted with things of your own? No one can serve two masters. For you will hate one and love the other; you will be devoted to one and despise the other. You cannot serve both God and money(italics mine). (Luke 16:9-13 NLT)

If you can't be faithful with a little, you can't be trusted with much! In other words, if you can't honor God when you have $10, you won't honor Him when you have $1,000, $10,000 or $100,000. So many young people fall into the deception that they can't honor God with the tithe (10 percent of their gross income) because they don't have enough money. In actuality, it is a test. God wants to see if He can trust you with a little bit so He can bless you with more! Moreover, if you haven't been faithful with something unrighteous, such as money, you won't be faithful with true riches (grace, blessings, promises, truth, revelation, spiritual things, souls, discipleship, and so forth). *Your handling of money is an indicator of whether or not you are qualified to handle "true riches" or spiritual things.*

R.G. LeTourneau was a famous Christian industrialist who used his wealth as a means to preach and fund the gospel. He was responsible for 299 different inventions, including the rubber tire, bulldozers, the portable crane, and the electric wheel. He also happened to be a multi-millionaire who *gave 90 percent to God and kept 10 percent to live on.* R.G. LeTourneau was convinced he could not out-give God. "I shovel it out," he would say, "and God shovels it back, but God has a bigger shovel."[2] Here is a man who knew why God had blessed Him with the ability to make money. He lived Matthew 6:33: "But seek first the kingdom and His righteousness and all these things shall be added to you."

God Owns It All

In order to handle money in a God honoring way, we must first understand this: *God owns it all and we are merely stewards.* One day, we will give an account of our stewardship over everything He has entrusted to us—money, family, ministry, relationships, words, and so forth (see Romans 14:12). David wrote, "The earth is the Lord's, *and all it contains,* the world, and those who dwell in it. (italics mine)" (Psalms 24:1-2 NASB). (Also see Leviticus 25:23, Haggai 2:8, 1 Corinthians 4:2, 1 Corinthians 6:19-20, and Deuteronomy 8:18).

Look at the definition of a steward: "A person who manages another's property or financial affairs; one who administers anything as the agent of another or others."[3] You are God's steward or manager. In fact, you really don't own anything at all: not your body, not your breath, and not your resources. According to this world, you may own things, but according the kingdom of God, you own nothing on this earth. Rather, you have been entrusted with these things. Understanding this principle will cause you to live differently and to think before making purchases. You will say, "God, do I really need this?" or "Is this a wise purchase?" or "Where can I invest these resources to advance Your kingdom?"

When you understand that God owns it all and He can give and take away, and when you understand that you can't take any of it with you when you die and that the only thing that will last are those things done with eternity in mind—then you will surrender "your" finances to God and your heart will follow! This makes the statement that you have only one Master, Jesus Christ. Moreover, worldly wealth secures heavenly treasures. Christ owns everything and we are co-heirs with Him! We are rewarded with rich heavenly treasures when we use earthly ones to advance His kingdom.

Money will try to master you, and as long as you only invest in earthly treasures, that's where your heart will be. When you invest in the kingdom of God, you are laying up for yourself treasure in heaven, and your heart will follow. *The issue is not how much money you make, but what you are doing with the resources that have been entrusted to you.* God is not interested in taking your money (which is really His money); He is interested in your heart. The reason He set up the system stewardship and generosity is so that money will not be our god. His desire is to bless us and have our hearts be wholly devoted to Him.

If you become a consistent giver, you will see a constant flow of provision given to you by God. God simply can't and wont be out-given. Robert Morris, author of *The Blessed Life,* has given away all of his possessions on several occasions, including his house and furniture, only to have it all back (and more) six months later! When you honor God with the first part of everything given to you, He honors you by taking care of all your needs.

Tithes and Offerings

Statistics tell us that only about 2-3% percent of Christians in America actually tithe and that giving per person is less today than it was during the Great Depression.[4] *Tithe* is a numerical word that literally means "a tenth." So the tithe refers to giving the *first* 10 percent of all your increase to the Lord.

> Honor the LORD with your wealth and with the *first fruits* of all your produce; then your barns will be filled with plenty, and your vats will be bursting with wine (italics mine). (Proverbs 3:9-10 ESV)

Tithing is primarily about honoring the Lord. When we give the Lord our first and best, or what the Bible calls the first fruits, this honors God. By doing so, we are acknowledging that He is the center of our lives. The term, *first fruits,* simply means "first in place, time, or order of rank, the chief, first, or principal thing."[5] So we give God our best right off the top. The tithe should be the first thing we give when we receive our pay check. God always wants our best. *He deserves it,* and He knows we need to have this principle in place in order to keep Him on the throne of our hearts! Anything less than Jesus being the center means we become self-focused. It's for our good. Every good thing we have is because God gave it to us (see James 1:17). The least we can do is honor Him with the first fruits.

In the Bible's first book, Genesis, we see the giving of first fruits practiced by Abel. Both Cain and Abel brought offerings to the Lord, but God accepted only one. Abel was a keeper of the sheep and Cain a worker of the ground. Cain brought "an offering of the fruit of the ground." Abel brought "of the *firstborn* of his flock and of their fat portions" (see Genesis 4:3-5). The story goes on to tell us that God accepted Abel's offering, but not Cain's. It doesn't tell us why, but it does say that Abel brought, "of the *firstborn* of his flock." Maybe Cain brought it as an afterthought, or gave God the leftovers? The issue may have been that God did not hold supremacy in Cain's heart. We all know what happened after that; Cain killed his brother Abel out of jealousy and rebellion because God accepted Abel's offering, but not his. God tried to help Cain and lead him toward repentance. I firmly believe had Cain repented and tried again, God would have accepted his offering. This practice of giving God the first fruits was set up from the very beginning, long before the Law of Moses. God knew that material things would compete for our supremacy in our hearts, so in His infinite wisdom, He established a way to ensure that wouldn't happen. That way is tithing and giving!

Tithing Is All About Honor

Tithes and offerings are two of the ways that we bring honor to God. All throughout the book of Malachi, God is talking to the priests. He goes through a whole list of things that they should be doing to honor Him but are not doing:

> A son honors his father, and a servant his master. Then if I am a father, where is My honor? And if I am a master, where is My respect?" says the LORD of hosts to you, O priests who despise My name. But you say, "How have we despised Your name?" (Malachi 1:6 NASB)

The passage goes on to say that they were giving God sacrifices that were blemished and lame when they were to be giving Him first and best. God asks them the question: "Would you give these to your governor?" (see Malachi 1:8).

It's kind of like when you have kids. You go to a restaurant as a special treat and buy them a burger and fries. When you ask for a French fry, the child complains. Finally, he relents and picks the puniest, wimpiest, burnt piece of potato he can find from underneath the pile. What the child fails to comprehend is that the parent was the one who bought the whole plate! Is this not an issue of honor and value? The child fails to comprehend the value of the person who has given them everything. The principle of the first is this: *surrendered worshipers have no trouble giving the first and best of that which they value most.*

One of the ways that children honor their fathers is through obedience. God doesn't need your money. He owns everything and lives in a city with streets of gold where precious gems are in abundance! The resources are to be used here on earth to advance His kingdom. Ministry takes money. The Church here on earth is meant to be the hands and feet of Jesus. The money is to be used to touch hurting people and take the gospel to the whole world.

Malachi 3:8 goes on to say that *we are robbing God if we refuse to give tithes and offerings.* That is a serious accusation—robbing God! I don't know about you, but if I say I love God and He is my Father, Lord, and Savior, I certainly don't want to be caught robbing Him. Do you rob people you say you love? If you say you love God and are robbing Him by not giving your tithe and offering, you had better rethink your commitment to Him. I would question whether or not your love for Him is real or just "fire insurance" in an attempt to clear your conscience.

God is deserving of every honor we can give Him. It is the least we can do for a God who gave His very own Son to take our sin upon Himself. He died a horrible death that we might have eternal life. Giving our tithes (10 percent) and offerings (whatever we determine that we can give cheerfully that will also stretch our faith) should come very easily considering the great length He has gone to in order to secure our eternal destinies.

Where Should I Give My Tithe?

Your tithe should go to your local church. If you don't have a local church, you should find one quickly! Your local church is the place where you are fed the Word of God and discipled (taught to love God, love others, and become like Christ). It's the place where you receive spiritual care and the soil in which you are planted. Maybe you say, "I don't feel very invested there." Jesus said our heart will follow our treasure (see Luke 12:34). If you invest your time, talents, and treasure there, your heart will follow. Our tithes and offerings are used to care for God's people, touch and impact the community and the world, care for the poor and needy, and provide for those pastors and leaders who watch out for your soul (see Hebrews 13:17). It just makes sense. There are conflicting views among pastors on what's called, "the storehouse principle" from Malachi 3:10, but in my mind it's a moot point. In the Old Testament, the storehouse was a part of the temple in Jerusalem. It was used to feed the Levites (those who ministered to the Lord) and take care of the poor, widows, and orphans. The people were to bring two tithes per year. Although I don't believe you can simply plug the New Testament Church into this passage I do think it's fair to say that the New Testament Church is a storehouse. It's a storehouse for the people of that particular body and for the community at hand. Resources are to be stored to feed the poor, reach out to the community and take care of those God has called to lead the local church. I don't feel it's at all inappropriate or unbiblical for pastors to ask for this. A true pastor is not asking so he can get rich. He is asking so you can be blessed (see Phillipians 4:17) and so the needs of people can be met. Tithes and offerings are God's system of blessing, and giving is a joy, not some crushing obligation meant to weigh us down.

> "Bring the whole tithe into the storehouse, so that there may be food in My house, and test Me now in this," says the LORD of hosts, "if I will not open for you the windows of heaven and pour out for you a blessing until it overflows." (Malachi 3:10 NASB)

To my knowledge, this is the only place in Scripture where God asks us to test Him. If you have never tried, I encourage you to tithe for six months and see what happens. I can guarantee you will be more blessed than you were before, and you won't even miss that money. Why? Because God said it! If at the end of that time you are more blessed that when you started, not just financially but in all ways, don't stop! If not, than by all means, stop! God is the one who said to test Him, not me.

The Tithe: A Floor Or a Ceiling?

Is the tithe to be the maximum of what we give? I don't believe so. What I love about the tithe is that it takes away the guesswork. It's a starting place for our giving. In my family, our personal goal was to start with the tithe and then increase our giving by percentage each year. We want to be extravagant givers. If your tithe goes to the local church, your offering should go wherever the Lord directs. That may be a missions fund in your church, a homeless shelter or ministry to the poor, a church building project, a missionary, or other ministries outside of your church where God directs you to give.

Blessed or Cursed? You Choose...

The prophet Malachi wrote this:

> "You are cursed with a curse, for you are robbing Me, the whole nation of you! (Malachi 3:9 NASB)

One of the ways the children of Israel had gone astray from God was in the practice of tithes and offerings. Those who do so are "cursed with the curse" the Scripture says. That doesn't sound very pleasant to me. It means to detest utterly, abhor, or abominate.[6] That's not something I want to be under! Galatians 3:13 reminds us Christ became a curse for us. Curses aren't for us to bear.

It's not something God does to you; it's something that happens because you have stepped out from under the shadow of His wing by not obeying His commands. Anytime you choose to disobey God and step outside the boundaries He has set up for your protection and good, you are taking matters into your own hands. If you have tried that before, you know it doesn't work. Think back to your life without God. Maybe you haven't lived long enough to figure out that life outside of God is a miserable thing. Maybe you are in the phase where you are dabbling in sin and it feels good. It only lasts for a season. One day you will realize that you are in a pig pen like the prodigal son and think, *I would be better off as a servant in my Father's house than I would here in this pig pen* (see Luke 15:15-17).

A Word on Grace Giving

I think grace giving is a great idea. Grace giving would say that a believer prays and does what the Lord asks of them. Although I've heard some use grace giving as a way to get out of giving altogether, others have a sincere heart in the matter. They are right in saying that for some, like a single mom with two jobs, 10% may be extremely difficult, but for others, 10% is a drop in the bucket. Yet I still believe that at least 10% is doable for many. It may be a stretch, you may have to adjust some things, it may take faith, but isn't that the point? In the end, you should still pray and obey. If you sincerely believe God is asking you to start at a lesser level and continue to raise the percentage, then be obedient to the Lord. My one word of advice would be this: don't stop at 10%! You will begin to find unparalleled fulfillment in your giving. For those earning larger sums of money, 10% may not even be a sacrifice. Grace gives us the power not only to keep the law but live beyond it (see Luke 21:1-8, Matt. 5:20-48, Matt. 23:23, 2 Cor. 8:1-3). In the end, I am not against grace giving, and I recognize there are times when it's valid to give less than 10%. God looks at the heart. If your heart is to "pray and obey" and that's where God is leading you, then do it. After all, obedience is better than sacrifice. Just don't use grace giving as an excuse not to give because you are stingy. And know this: God may ask you to give above and beyond the tithe as you pray and obey. In the end, if you are conflicted on the issue, just start with the tithe and remove the guesswork. You will be glad you did!

Where to Start

Maybe you are wondering where to start with your money? I like some of Dave Ramsey's "Seven Baby Steps" for getting out of debt, but have modified them slightly:[7]

1. *Start giving your tithe.* The tithe is 10 percent of your income, and offerings are anything beyond that. Even if you make $10 per week, the tithe is your honor to God. When you give the tithe, the rest of your money is blessed!
2. *Start a budget.*
3. *Save $1,000 in an emergency fund.*
4. *Pay off all debt with the debt snowball.* Start with the lowest debt first, and pay it off. Then put that amount toward the next debt, in addition to what you were already paying.
5. *Expand your emergency fund to three-to-six months' worth of expenses.*
6. *Start giving offerings in addition to the tithe.*
7. *Invest*

I have included a sample of the budget I use in Appendix E. There are also several good money programs for your computer if that works better for you. Feel free to adjust it as needed. Obviously, I haven't given you a comprehensive view on money management. For additional reading, see the resource list at the end of the chapter.

Discussion Questions

1. If you are in college or plan on attending college, why? (Be honest!)
2. Did you come to a new understanding of tithing and giving? Explain.
3. Will you make a commitment to start tithing and giving regardless of how little or how much money you are making right now?
4. Do you have a budget? If not, please make one by next week.
5. Do you have an emergency fund or any other savings? If not, make sure it's top priority right after tithing in your budget.

Resources

Appendix E: Sample Monthly Budget
In God We Trust by Bob Santos
The Blessed Life by Robert Morris
Money and the Christian by Caleb McAffe
Debt Free Living by Larry Burkett
The Treasure Principle by Randy Alcorn
Money, Possessions and Eternity by Randy Alcorn
Quicken money management program - www.quicken.intuit.com

Meditation Verse

Honor the LORD with your possessions, and with the first fruits of all your increase; so your barns will be filled with plenty, and your vats will overflow with new wine. (Proverbs 3:9-10 NKJV)

PART 6

FINDING AND FULFILLING YOUR PURPOSE

Jesus told His followers, "It's to your advantage that I go away, for if I do not go away, the helper will not come to you. But if I go, I will send Him to you" (John 16:7 ESV). The person and power of the Holy Spirit helps us discover God's will and empowers us to carry it out. As you navigate your college years, being filled with the Holy Spirit, finding your purpose, and carrying it out are essential.

CHAPTER 14

YOU NEED POWER

I labored over whether or not to put this chapter in the book because of all the differences in opinion about the ministry of the Holy Spirit, but in the end I decided the book wouldn't be complete without it. The ministry of the Holy Spirit has been too valuable in my life and in the lives of millions of believers to skip over it. This isn't meant to be an argument, but rather a testimony of His goodness and power in my life and the lives of millions of believers worldwide who have had a similar experience. For our purposes, I will call it *the baptism of the Holy Spirit* (see Matthew 3:11, Mark 1:8, Luke 3:16, John 1:33). On some things, I will remain intentionally vague. Rather than a full and detailed explanation, the aim of this chapter is to let the believer know there is power available to you should you want it. While some may be irritated that I haven't said enough, others may think I'm assuming too much. With that in mind, let's begin.

When I came to Christ in 1996, I came with tons of baggage. But as you have probably discovered, baggage doesn't just instantly fall off. Although we are new creations *in Christ* when we are born again, our full potential is something we realize and grow into. Otherwise, we would be "Super Christians" the moment we are born again. Let me just make a few introductory comments up front to put you at ease:

- You experience the indwelling of the Holy Spirit when you are saved.
- There is no question that all true believers, "baptized in the Holy Spirit" or not, will go to heaven. In other words, speaking in tongues is not a golden ticket into heaven. Salvation is by grace through faith; that is, relationship with God through

the shed blood of Jesus Christ is what determines whether or not you spend eternity with Jesus. Your name must be written in the Lamb's Book of Life, period (see Rev. 21:27).

- No Christians are sub-par based on whether or not they have experienced the baptism in the Holy Spirit. Conversely, those who have been baptized in the Holy Spirit are not super Christians. *There are no classes of Christians.* We are all sons and daughters of the King.

Hopefully, this puts your mind at ease so you can read with an open heart. Of course, you may be from a background, as I was, where you didn't really hear anything about the baptism of the Holy Spirit. In that case, you are in a good place, as you don't have to labor through confusion over what you were taught or not taught.

Back to my story. After coming to Christ in 1996, I struggled significantly for another two years. I couldn't seem to overcome certain sin habits that ruled my life. I just didn't have the power! So one night during a mid-week service at my church, our pastor was preaching about being "baptized in the Holy Spirit."

You can call it an infilling, an additional filling, or whatever you like; it doesn't matter to me. I just know something changed. My pastor went through a biblical account concerning what it means to be baptized in or with the Holy Spirit. It didn't take much for me to decide that I wanted what he was talking about! So I received this baptism the same way I received salvation – by grace through faith (see Ephesians 2:8-10, Romans 5:2 and Colossians 2:6).

The following week, I was out at a nightclub with some friends (a normal occurrence for me at that time). They were all out on the dance floor drinking and dancing, but that night I happened to stay back. This was rare because I loved to dance. As I was sitting on a bar stool in the corner, I began to have a sick feeling in the pit of my stomach. Not an upset stomach, but more like a deep disgust. I suddenly came to realize the type of darkness I was participating in and I said to myself, "What am I doing here? I don't belong here!" You see, I wasn't at the bar to be a light for Christ. I was there because it had been an identity for me, a place to carry out evil and sinful desires. I walked out of the bar that night never to go back to my old lifestyle. For me, the bar had been a place of unbreakable sin habits like lust and drunkenness. Not only that, but after quitting the bar scene I was also able to quit smoking. Although it was only a cigarette a day, I just couldn't seem to let it go before this happened.

After receiving this baptism in the Holy Spirit, I began to experience a new power and boldness to share my faith. There was also an openness and receptivity to spiritual gifts. I began to have more discernment of spiritual things and walk in spiritual gifts such as tongues and interpretation, words of wisdom and knowledge, as well as prophecy (see 1 Corinthians 12 and 14).

The Holy Spirit Is a Person

It's very important to understand that the *Holy Spirit is a person*. The baptism in the Holy Spirit is not primarily about speaking in tongues or operating in spiritual gifts. First and foremost, it's about a deeper relationship with the person of the Holy Spirit. He is God, and just as much as the Father and Jesus want a relationship with us, so does the Holy Spirit! The baptism in the Holy Spirit gave me a deeper relationship with and a greater sensitivity to the Person of the Holy Spirit.

Jesus Needed the Holy Spirit

Jesus needed the Holy Spirit while He walked this earth. Remember, Jesus was fully God, yet fully man (see Colossians 2:9-10). That means He had to rely on the Holy Spirit to lead and guide Him. Jesus ministered through the power and leading of the Holy Spirit. He set the example for how we are to live and walk by the Spirit. He was empowered with the Holy Spirit since birth, otherwise He wouldn't have remained sinless (that takes Holy Spirit power). But something new happened after He was baptized by John the Baptist.

In John 1:32, after being baptized, John said this about Jesus: "I have seen the Spirit descending as a dove out of heaven, and He *remained* upon Him." However you view it, something happened to Jesus that day, because afterward He started His powerful public ministry. That word *remained* is the

Greek word *meno*. It's the same word used in John 15:1-6 when it talks about abiding or dwelling in the vine. It means, "to stay (in a given place, state, relation, or expectancy) abide, continue, dwell, endure, be present, stand, or tarry."[1] If Jesus needed an abiding, enduring relationship with the Holy Spirit in this way to be successful in fulfilling the Father's will on this earth, how much more do we need the Holy Spirit! God wants us "clothed with power from on high" in order to accomplish His purpose and calling (see Luke 24:49).

The same thing happened with the disciples after Jesus died and rose again. In John 20:22, it says Jesus breathed on them, and said to them, "Receive the Holy Spirit." Why then does He tell them in Acts 1:5 that they would be "Baptized with the Holy Spirit not many days from now?" It's after this baptism that tongues of fire appear, they all speak in a language they never learned, and several thousand people are added to the kingdom of God in a single day (see Acts 2). Now that's power! The disciples then walk in supernatural power from that point on. This power wasn't exclusively for the first generation of apostles. Nowhere in Scripture is that mentioned. On the contrary, Peter says of this power, "... for the promise is for you and for your children and for *all* who are afar off, everyone whom the Lord our God calls for Himself" (Acts 2:38-39). If this Holy Spirit baptism was only for the first-generation apostles, we are in trouble! In my opinion, it's just a convenient way to explain why the Church at large (at least in certain parts of the world) doesn't have much power. I personally need the Holy Spirit every bit as much (and probably more) than the first-generation apostles needed the Him!

The baptism in the Holy Spirit is primarily given to empower the believer to *be* witnesses and to *do* the works God has called us to do. This is what happened in Jesus' life, in the lives of countless believers throughout the generations, and in my life. When studying Church history, the baptism of the Holy Spirit never totally disappeared. Although not as apparent, prominent Church figures throughout history make mention of it. In his book, *Charismatic Gifts in the Early Church,* Professor Ronald Kydd:

"We find clear evidence of their use (the baptism and gifts) in the *Didache* (otherwise known as "The Teaching of the Twelve Apostles'), the writings of Clement of Rome, Ignatius, Hermas (the 'Shepherd'), Justin Martyr, Celsus, Irenaeus, Eusebius of Caesarea, Theodotus, Hippolytus, Novatian, Tertullian, Cyprian, Origen, Dionysius, Firmilian."

He goes on to say, "There came a point around AD 260 at which they (baptism and gifts) no longer fitted the highly organized, well-educated, wealthy, socially powerful Christian communities."[2]

The Evidence of the Holy Spirit

The primary evidence that we have the Holy Spirit actively involved in our lives is the fruit of the Spirit (see Gal. 5:22-23), not speaking in tongues. I personally don't have a problem with speaking in tongues. In fact, I do it every day. Speaking in tongues is meant to personally edify us, build us up, or charge us up like a battery (see Jude 20). The problem is many of us know someone who speaks in tongues, but lives like the devil, who is prideful about this experience or who is flippant about the way they use this gift. The thing to remember is that the *spiritual gifts are no guarantee of spiritual maturity.* How do I know this? Just look at the Corinthians! They had all the gifts yet they were extremely immature. It's the fruit of the Spirit, not the gifts, that is the true evidence of being empowered by and filled with the Holy Spirit. Yet that still doesn't negate the need for spiritual gifts. Many times throughout Scripture, speaking in tongues and prophesying were the evidence of having received the baptism in the Holy Spirit in the way we are talking about (see Acts 8:1-19; 10:44-46, 19:1-6). Can someone be filled with the Holy Spirit and not speak in tongues? I'm sure this is the case. Nonetheless, these cases represented in Acts are very interesting and point to the importance of tongues and prophecy in connection with the baptism of the Spirit.

One of the most interesting and poignant cases that point to the baptism of the Holy Spirit being a separate and needed experience is found in Acts 8. As the story goes, Philip had preached the gospel in Samaria, and the people received it with joy and were baptized. So there was no question that these people had put their trust in the Lord Jesus Christ and were saved. Why then were Peter and John sent to pray for them to receive the Holy Spirit after this happened?

> Now when the apostles at Jerusalem heard that Samaria had received the word of God, they sent to them Peter and John, who came down and prayed for them that they might receive the Holy Spirit, for he had not yet fallen on any of them, but they had only been baptized in the name of the Lord Jesus. (Acts 8:14-16 ESV)

It seems that this was a usual occurrence in the early church. People were baptized in the name of the Lord Jesus *and* baptized in the Holy Spirit. In the end, I think we can all agree: Christians need power! If you lack power, all you have to do is ask God for it. Jesus said, "So if you sinful people know how to give good gifts to your children, how much more will your heavenly Father give the Holy Spirit to those who ask Him" (Luke 11:13 NLT). God doesn't want you to lead a powerless life, constantly struggling with sin habits, addictions, and bondages and thinking that you can never be free. He wants you to experience Him in the fullest sense. He wants you to have power!

> But you will receive *power* when the Holy Spirit comes upon you. And you will *be* My witnesses, telling people about Me everywhere—in Jerusalem, throughout Judea, in Samaria, and to the ends of the earth (italics mine). (Acts 1:8 NLT)

The baptism of the Holy Spirit is primarily about living as a witness, personal empowerment over sin, and the miracle working power of Christ. It is the gateway into the manifestation gifts given to us in 1 Corinthians 12. The word *power* from Acts 1:8 is the Greek word *dunamis*. It means:

Force (literally or figuratively); *specifically miraculous power*, ability, abundance, meaning, might, power, strength, violence, mighty (wonderful) work.[3]

I don't know about you, but I need that! It is the power to live godly, preach the gospel, be bold, see signs, wonders, and miracles happen, and *be* and *live* as witnesses (the word also means martyrs) for Jesus. You need power on your college campus. You need power in your job. You need power in your family. You need power to *be* a witness. I like what one minister said concerning this:

"The primary purpose of the Holy Spirit infilling is to continually receive supernatural power to be God's witnesses regarding the coming kingdom of heaven."[4]

In fact, we haven't fully preached the gospel until it's been done with power! Paul wrote:

For I will not dare to speak of any of those things which Christ has not accomplished through me, in word and deed, to make the Gentiles obedient—*in mighty signs and wonders, by the power of the Spirit of God,*

> so that from Jerusalem and round about to Illyricum
> *I have fully preached the gospel of Christ* (italics mine).
> (Romans 15:18-19)

The gospel is preached through both word and deed. How many of us have ever really seen the power of God? We have seen a lot of slick presentations, but what we need is power. We need the mighty saving power of Christ. We need healing. We need deliverance. We need the supernatural gifts. The world is waiting for this.

In the end, you may agree or disagree with me. But what no one can disagree with is the power and impact this experience had on Christ's disciples, on millions of believers throughout history, and in my personal walk with God. It was after I was baptized in the Holy Spirit that I was able to live what I talked, be a bold witness, walk in supernatural gifts, be empowered for ministry, and overcome sin habits that had previously held me captive. For me and countless others, this has been a life-altering experience. I pray it can be for you too!

How to Receive the Holy Spirit

1. Repent of sin—especially hidden sin and unforgiveness (see Matthew 6:14-15).
2. Ask God for the Holy Spirit (see Luke 11:13).
3. Receive the Spirit by faith (see Romans 5:2).
4. Open your mouth and speak by faith. Many times when people received the baptism of the Holy Spirit, they spoke in tongues and prophesied. Speaking in tongues is a supernatural language that you don't know. God won't move your lips for you; you must open your mouth and He will fill it. Like everything else in the kingdom, it must be by faith (see Acts 2:4).
5. Have someone who has had this experience lay hands on you and pray for you to receive it (see Acts 19:6).

Discussion Questions

1. What is your experience with the Holy Spirit?
2. Is there evidence of the fruit of the Spirit in your life (check against Galatians 5:22-23)?
3. Do you need more power in your life? Are you willing to ask for it?
4. Go ahead, just ask Him. The Father loves to give the Holy Spirit to those who ask Him (see Luke 11:13).

Resources

A Handbook on Holy Spirit Baptism by Don Basham
How to be Filled with the Holy Spirit by A.W. Tozer
The Skeptics Guide to Tongues and Prophecy by Peter Haas
– download for free at http://www.peterhaas.org/wp-content/uploads/2015/04/SkepticsGuideToTongues2015.pdf (Peter is the pastor of Substance Church in Roseville, MN.)

Meditation Verses

Keep on asking, and you will receive what you ask for. Keep on seeking, and you will find. Keep on knocking, and the door will be opened to you. (Matthew 7:7 NLT)

So if you sinful people know how to give good gifts to your children, how much more will your heavenly Father give the Holy Spirit to those who ask Him. (Luke 11:13 NLT)

But you will receive power when the Holy Spirit comes on you; and you will be my witnesses in Jerusalem, and in all Judea and Samaria, and to the ends of the earth. (Acts 1:8 NIV)

CHAPTER 15

FINDING YOUR PURPOSE

Discovering your purpose can be frustrating for young people in their late teens and early twenties. We all feel this and know deep in our hearts there is more to life than we are living, and yet we don't always know how to get there. Some people search all their lives and never find their purpose. It should not be so with the children of God. I'm not saying you will always see it clearly, but if you are following hard after God, He will begin to put you on the scent early in your walk with Him.

When I was a baby Christian, barely two months into my walk with God, I woke up out of bed one morning and suddenly knew that I was called to be a minister of the gospel. I didn't know when, where, or how, but I knew His call for my life.

God isn't trying to hide your purpose from us; He wants us to know our purpose. He longs for us to know His good, pleasing, and perfect will (see Romans 12:1-2) even more than we long to know it. As we find His will, we also find our purpose. Ephesians 2:10 says, "For we are his workmanship, created in Christ Jesus for good works, which God prepared beforehand, that we should walk in them."

Do you see it? You should be getting very excited right now! You were created for *good* works, *which God prepared beforehand* (to fit up in advance, prepare before)[1] *for you to walk in!* God crafted you for good works before the foundation of the world. Why would He try to hide that from you? That would be like making a masterpiece and hiding it in the basement with a cloth over it! No, when He created the world, He had you in mind. He had specific good works that needed to be done, and He crafted you exactly and precisely to carry out those good works. Your life has purpose and destiny written all over it! To live life for any other reason than God's pleasure is to sell yourself short of God's best.

Hide and Seek with God

I once heard pastor and author Tommy Tenney give an example of how God plays "hide-and-seek" with us. It's kind of like a dad playing hide-and-seek with his small children. Daddy hides, but sticks out His foot just enough so His children can see it!

One day I was riding bikes with my son around a local trail when we came upon a short series of 90-degree turns that put me out of his sight. Although I was only twenty or so feet ahead of him, he couldn't see me. As I sped up through the turns I could hear him saying, "Daddy, wait! Where are you! I can't see you! Where are we going? Daddy, stop! Are we going to get ice cream? You are going too fast!" I waited for him and when he caught up, I said, "Kole, I'm right here. Just follow me!" Suddenly I knew what God must feel like. He is always there, sometimes just up ahead, around a curve or barely out of sight. We get so nervous and scared thinking He has left us or doesn't care, when in reality He is right there saying, "I'm right here. Just follow Me."

We have a good Daddy. He is not trying to hide Himself or His will from us, but He does want us to seek Him and discover it. After all, He promises that when we seek, we will find (see Matthew 7:7-8). Part of the joy of seeking is finding, but He doesn't reveal everything all at once. It's a step-by-step process of discovery. We seek Him for each step and when He reveals it to us, we take the step directly in front of us. If we are not obedient to that step, why would God reveal the next one? We often want to bypass the easy small steps and cut to the chase, but that's not how God works. It's a bit like the movie, *Raiders of the Lost Ark*. In that movie, when Indiana Jones finally comes near to the Holy Grail, there is one last chasm between him and the cup. In order to get it, he has to step off the cliff, trusting that there is an invisible bridge to catch his foot when he steps. Faith sometimes feels like that. I've heard it said, "Faith inch by inch is a cinch, but mile by mile is a trial." God prepares and strengthens our faith by taking us one step at a time, even if we can't see how each step ties together. Getting from point A to point B in God's kingdom is never a straight line; it's more like a zigzag, or better yet, a road with twists and turns. It's an exciting journey. As we step from stone to stone, we will look back over several years and see God's hand of providence in our journey. *God progressively builds upon what He has been doing in our lives.*

Sometimes the steps are faith are easy, and sometimes they are hard, but they all require faith. As God builds our faith and trust in Him, He allows us to take bigger and bigger steps of faith, and the underlying reason for the whole process is getting to know Him along the way. Reaching the destination is sweet, but it's not the goal. Jesus, not the task, is the final destination. One day, we will stand before Jesus face to face and know Him just as we are known (see 1 Corinthians 13:12).

The only journey I can give you is my own. In the beginning of the chapter, I told you how I knew very early on in my walk with Christ that I was called to be a pastor, although I didn't know what the journey would look like or what it would require. In fact, I thought I was ready to be "in the ministry" much earlier than God thought I was ready. After college, I worked five different jobs while faithfully serving at my church. I served as a youth worker, usher, worship leader, youth pastor, college pastor, and occasional preacher. At one point, I remember going to my pastor and saying, "I think it's time for me to step out into ministry." The only problem was there was nothing to step into! I didn't have a word from the Lord, I didn't have a position offered to me, nor did I even have a vision for exactly what I was going to do, but I was ready!

Thank God my pastor was wiser and more experienced than I was. He told me to just continue working and volunteering at the church, because it wasn't time for this step. It was another four-to-five years before God opened up the door for me to step into my calling. When the door did open, God had prepared us to become full-time missionaries where we would have to trust the Lord for our entire income. Tough financial times at the beginning of our marriage were the means God used to prepare us for this bigger financial step. Years of working in youth ministry and then pioneering a college and career ministry prepared me for the specific ministry role as the director of a whole network of campus ministries called BASIC.

Then, after four years of doing that, the Lord called us to take the biggest step of our lives. He began to speak to us that "transition was coming." After seeking Him for more than a year, He spoke to us from this passage:

> Now the LORD said to Abram, "Go forth from your country, and from your relatives and from your father's house, to the land which I will show you; and I will make you a great nation, and I will bless you, and make your name great; and so you shall be a blessing". (Genesis 12:1-2 NASB)

Every time we tried to think beyond this one step, "Go forth from your country, and from your relatives and your father's house (or that which is familiar and comfortable), to the land which I will show you," we would become anxious and confused. Finally, we gave up trying to know all the answers and came to the point of trusting like children. We put in our one-year resignation notice with BASIC. We were on a new journey and we didn't know what was coming next!

I had many months of anxiety and worry over this. I am a visionary person and tend to have big-picture vision, but the only thing I could see in this case was the step directly in front of us. For me, not knowing where we were going was a huge step. All the typical feelings you would expect came into play: fear, anxiety, worry, and the like. The only thing that gave me assurance was gazing into the eyes of Jesus in my personal prayer time. When I did this, I knew we were doing the right thing. It wasn't until nearly five months later, the Lord made it clear that we were to move to Cambridge, Massachusetts, to plant a church near Harvard University.

God's Good Purpose

We need to trust in the goodness of the Lord. He has our best interest in mind, and it is wrapped up in His best interest. We find our purpose in His plan! "I know the plans that I have for you, declares the LORD. They are plans for peace and not disaster, plans to give you a future filled with hope" (Jeremiah 29:11 GW).

I often say, "The best place to be is exactly where God wants you!" Whether that's an igloo in Alaska, a mansion in Hollywood, a hut in the jungle, or a house in suburbia, there is no replacement for being in the center of His will. Wherever He has places us is our place of blessing! Remember, God called Abraham to a specific land, and He calls us to specific places for our good and the good of the people who are there.

If you are in college because you felt God placed you there, you are in the right place. If you are there because you simply want to pursue the American dream, maybe you need to shift gears and trust Him with your life. We must deeply consider the words that Jesus said, "Whoever finds His life will lose it, and whoever loses his life for my sake will find it" (Matthew 10:39).

We often have a hard time trusting God. Many of us don't trust His plan for our lives. Our self-centeredness exposes this lack of trust. Do we make decisions based solely on how it will affect us, or do we make decisions based on His will and the good of other people? You will be most fulfilled when you fulfill God's best interest for your life! Why? Because He created you to fulfill His purpose.

If you can't find that purpose, it's because you aren't looking. Maybe you are unwilling to surrender full control of your life to Jesus. Wherever we are, we should be all there. Focus on Him and throw your life wholeheartedly and recklessly into relationship with Him and His plan and purpose. If you don't know what that is, just start seeking to know Him wholeheartedly and serving God and others selflessly, and you will probably find it!

When I was just out of college, I was working at a gas station. To make matters worse, I had the first shift, which meant I had to open up the store at 5A.M.. That meant I had to get up at about 4 a.m., a difficult task for someone just out of college. One morning I was looking out the window, drawing a picture of the bridge nearby, when I heard someone wildly banging on the window. It was my boss. Apparently, a customer had been sitting at the full-serve pump for several minutes and I hadn't noticed! Talk about an unfulfilling job. It definitely wasn't my dream job. In my mind, I hadn't spent four and a half years in college to work at a gas station in Eldred, Pennsylvania! Eventually they let me go because they didn't need me anymore (another story for another time), but my point is this: though it wasn't my dream job or what I knew I had been called to do, I learned to be content. I continued to carry in my heart the dream and vision for which He created me and sought day by day to follow Him. I threw myself wholeheartedly into my relationship with God and into serving others through my local church. I never let my dream to preach the gospel and lead people into deeper relationship with Jesus escape. The Book of Proverbs says it this way:

> Where there is no prophetic vision, people cast off restraint. (Proverbs 29:18)

There was also a quote by Howard Thurman that I memorized and would recite often:

> Don't ask yourself what the world needs, ask yourself what makes you come alive and go do that, because what the world needs is people who have come alive!

I am still in the same place today. Although I am doing what I was created to do, I still have dreams and visions that are unfulfilled. I am walking with Jesus step by step and learning to be content while the dreams come to pass, always keeping them in my vision, but allowing God to work out in His time and way. As my friend says, *look ahead but don't live ahead!*[2]

Conclusion and Discussion Questions

God will give you glimpses of the "big picture," but what you should be concerned about at this moment are these two questions in regard to your purpose:

1. Am I developing into the person God wants me to be? Have I defined the person God wants me to be (define who you want to be before you define what you want to do).
2. What is the step directly in front of me that God is asking me to take?
3. Am I where God wants me to be at this point in my life?
4. It's OK to form plans based on God's leading. Take this week to pray, get an idea of the desires God has put inside of you (see Psalms 37:4), and formulate a tentative plan based on that. What are your dreams and desires? If there were nothing to hinder you, what would you do with God?

We should focus more on who we are becoming than what we are doing. At the end of the day, we will be remembered for who we were more than what we did. If you know God has called you to be right where you are, rest in that, do what you are doing, and trust God to show you the steps. Then take them as they come. If you don't know where you are supposed to be, stay where you are until you have some clear direction. If you are walking with God in an intimate relationship, it will be hard to miss His direction and purpose for your life!

Meditation Verses

> Trust in the LORD with all your heart and do not lean on your own understanding. In all your ways acknowledge Him, and He will make your paths straight. (Proverbs 3:5-6 NASB)

CHAPTER 16

GO!

So many students and young adults either have a mediocre vision for their college years or no vision at all. This is not about simply staying Christian in college or young adulthood. Nor is it simply about doing well in your studies, though you should strive to do your best. *You are also there to make a difference and help lead others into a life-giving relationship with Jesus Christ!* College is often a "last stop" for people on their journey of faith. The older people get, the less likely they are to come into relationship with Christ. Don't waste four-to-eight years of your life by thinking you are *only* there to study. This would be a grave mistake. You are there to fulfill part of God's dream and vision for your life (see Habakuk 2:2; Ephesians 3:20). It doesn't have to wait until after college. In fact, it already began before you were born. If you are there as a Christian simply to get a degree so you can make a lot of money and live the American dream, you need a vision adjustment. You are a missionary, a minister of reconciliation, and an ambassador for Jesus. You never know who you may have the opportunity to influence at college. You could be talking to a future senator, Supreme Court justice, president, superintendent, actor, sports star, and so forth. Maybe you will even fall into one of these categories yourself. The university in my back yard, Harvard, has seen eight United States presidents come from her. The question is, what will you do with the influence you are given?

As I quoted before, Walt Henrichsen, author of *Disciples Are Made Not Born,* said, "If you are at college for any other reason than to be a missionary for Jesus Christ, you are there for selfish, sinful reasons."[1] Too many people go to college for the almighty "I." It's all about a good job, what *I* want out of life or what's best for *me*. What about what's best for God and His kingdom? God's principle is clear: "Seek first the kingdom of God and His righteousness and all these things will be added unto you" (see Matthew 6:33). We are not living for or unto ourselves nor are we living for our own glory. The purpose for every believer is the same: to glorify God and esteem others better than yourself. Pastor John Piper says it like this: "The chief end of man is to glorify God by enjoying Him forever. God is most glorified in us when we are most satisfied in Him."[1] When we take the focus off ourselves and find our pleasure in God and His will, we are able to live for His purposes and willingly lay down our lives for Him and for others. We will go wherever He wants us to go and do whatever He wants us to do, not out of duty, but out of delight.

Vision

God has a vision for your life. Your job is to search it out to find what it is. It directs us, keeps us, and motivates us to follow Him regardless of the cost. Listen to the wisdom of His Word. "Where there is no prophetic vision the people cast off restraint, but blessed is he who keeps the law" (Proverbs 29:18 ESV). Without vision–God revealing prophetic insight and revelation to us–we run wild. His vision is like having the bumpers up when you go bowling: it keeps our lives from going into the gutter.

To the best of your ability, write down God's vision for your life, and if you are in college, particularly for your college experience. Start with what you know. Maybe take some time, find a secret place and pray about it. Here are a few questions you can ask Him:

- Who do You want me to be? (It's always better to first define the type of person you want to be.)
- Why am I here? In college, on the earth, etc...
- What am I good at?
- Who am I here to impact?
- Who have You called to walk with me?
- What church and campus ministry do You want me involved in? (Remember, you can't do it alone.)

When you write down your vision and look at it often, it should send you to your knees because you realize it is too beg for you to accomplish without divine intervention and other people. It should inspire you and others.

> Then the LORD told me: "I will give you my message in the form of a vision (dream, revelation, oracle). Write it clearly enough to be read at a glance. At the time I have decided, my words will come true. You can trust what I say about the future. It may take a long time, but keep on waiting—it will happen." (Habakkuk 2:2-3 CEV)

Late author Steven Covey says, "Begin with the end in mind."[2] Beginning with the end in mind will cause you to start from a different vantage point. A small adjustment now means a huge change later! Right now you may be accomplishing very little of your vision. It may seem like it will never come, but small investments made early pay big dividends down the road. Vision reminds you why you are doing what you are doing, and keeps you on the right path. It limits your life to what matters. Vision encourages you when times get tough, when you don't want to continue, when you have had enough of school, when you are criticized, when hurt and pain come, and when you have to sacrifice. That written vision of what God has put in your heart makes the goal clear. You see the end result and say, "It's all worth it!" Jesus began with the end in mind. Listen what Paul said about Him: "Who for the joy that was set before Him endured the cross" (Hebrews 12:2). What was the joy set before Him? Giving His Father glory by freeing all mankind from the slavery of sin and providing a way for them to come into relationship with Him. You endure the pain, hardship, and sacrifice for the joy set before you—the end result! Vision is what it will look like when all is said and done!

Vision should be simple and clear so that it can be seen at a glance. Here are some examples:

- To develop a cure for cancer in my lifetime
- To lead a generation in the worship and adoration of God (that's one of mine)
- To become a godly Supreme Court justice
- To own my own company that funds the preaching of the gospel on the earth
- To give away 25 million dollars in my lifetime
- To see abortion ended in my lifetime
- To provide health care for every man, woman, and child in America
- To be a godly and righteous politician
- To bring excellent education to urban school districts
- To help third-world children get the best education possible.

Lastly, when we write the vision, it will inspire someone else's life—"so that he may run who reads it" (see Habakkuk 2:2). I really like how this commentary explains it: "so intelligible as to be easily read by any one running past."[3] It has to be plain. It has to be clear. It has to be big. Vision gives people wings. It causes them to want to join you and have a vision for their own lives.

Destiny

Believers in Jesus have a destiny, and that destiny is inextricably linked to other people. How do you view your time in college? Is it to have fun, study, or get involved in student government? It could include all of those things, but you must have the big picture first: *you are there for the glory of God.* That could play out many different ways, but one of the ways it surely plays out is that *you are not in college for yourself. You must look at your college campus as your mission field. You must look outside of yourself.* God didn't plant you there just so you could study, have fun, get involved in as many student activities as possible, or make a lot of money upon graduation.

Don't miss the big picture. *You are there to impact those around you!* You are there to change the culture of the campus, to bring the kingdom of God to earth, and to see lives changed for eternity. You have a unique four-year opportunity to impact your friends and campus with the gospel of Jesus Christ. The point isn't just to stay Christian in college; that's just the beginning. The point is to thrive in your faith, to find your calling, and to change your campus. It's impossible to thrive in your faith if you are totally focused on yourself. God's principle is clear: "Give and it shall be given to you" (Luke 6:38). Our Savior also said, "It is more blessed to give than receive" (Acts 20:35).

I call it the overflowing cup principle. The overflowing cup principle is this: *You can only be filled to overflowing when you pour out to others.* Let's look at it a little more in depth:

He who believes in Me, as the Scripture said, "From his innermost being will flow **rivers** of living water." (John 7:38 NASB)

But whoever drinks of the water that I will give him shall never thirst; but the water that I will give him will become in him a well of water springing up to eternal life. (John 4:14 NASB)

A thief comes only to rob, kill, and destroy. I came so that everyone would have life, and have it in its fullest (*superabundant, excessive, superior*)(italics mine). (John 10:10 CEV)

Rivers and fountains are always flowing. *If we do not give out, God cannot fill us to overflowing.* Many Christians are satisfied to live their lives with a full cup instead of an overflowing one. They are filled up with God and are satisfied to live that way; after all, it's better than being empty. But there is another level God wants believers to graduate into. It's overflow. This only happens when we give out to others that which God has given to us. When we are continually giving out, God can continually pour back in. That means there is a flow like a river or a fountain coming from the depths of our beings. As we pour out in abundance, God pours in even more! Please don't misunderstand me; this doesn't mean we don't need any rest or relaxation. It just means we are to live a lifestyle of "pouring out."

It works like this: we become intimate with Jesus, He begins to fill us, and as we give out, it becomes a flow. We go back to Jesus: He fills us to overflowing, we pour out... and on and on. We can never replace abiding in Jesus with "doing." Abiding and giving out are to go hand in hand. This was the model of Jesus' life. He often got up earlier than everyone else or withdrew to the wilderness to pray. He would then pour out to the multitudes. It was the overflowing cup principle! Our identity and fruit comes from abiding in Him, knowing Him intimately, hearing His heartbeat, and being obedient to that which He says (see John 15). When we do this, we begin to overflow, and we can't stop ourselves from pouring out.

Why is there so much emphasis right now among your generation on living for something bigger than yourself? From opposing the sex-slave trade to providing people with clean water, people are thinking outside of themselves. I believe followers of Jesus are the ones to lead the way in seeing our world changed. The difference is, we do it by Christ and for Christ. When Christ enters the equation, it is elevated from a good thing or simply a humanitarian effort to a divine effort that's meant to introduce Jesus to the world and has eternal ramifications.

Seeing Your Campus as a Mission Field

Your campus is *your* mission field. The situation is dire. Less than 5 percent of people on your college campus are followers of Jesus, but whether it's your university, your job, your family, your friends, or another area—*God has called you to have an outward focus.* As a follower of Jesus, you will never be satisfied living life for yourself. Remember, God so loved the world that He gave...

In the beginning of the chapter, I asked the question, what

brings God glory? There are many things that bring God glory, but answer this question honestly: Do you think it would bring God glory for you to personally prosper in your faith, but keep it to yourself? Do you really have a vibrant faith if you aren't concerned about those all around you who don't know Jesus?

The best definition I have ever heard for love is this: "Love is living for the good of others."[4] This type of love, the God kind of love, must permeate everything we do. It must be so ingrained in us that we naturally give out wherever we are. We can't do it on our own; it has to be God-empowered. We love because He first loved us (see 1 John 4:19). We must experience His love and then give it away.

Earlier I quoted Acts 20:35 "It's more blessed to give than receive." It's true. It's only in our giving out that we are filled to overflowing. In Luke 10, Jesus sent out seventy of His disciples two by two into every city where He Himself was about to go. They were to heal the sick and declare the kingdom of God. When they returned, they returned with joy (see Luke 10:17). Whether I'm on an out-of-town ministry trip, ministering at my local church, in a small group, ministering to a friend, or doing street evangelism—without fail, I return with joy! There is something about pouring out that gives us joy and fills us up! In fact, I believe living an outward-focused life is as much for the joy of the follower of Jesus as it is for those who don't know Jesus.

Love for the Lost

I recently heard it said, "The Church is the only organization whose members are to live for the non-members."[5] If we are intimate with Jesus and lay our heads on His breast as the apostle John did, we will hear the heartbeat of heaven and know that God loves lost people:

For the Son of Man has come to seek and to save that which was lost. (Luke 19:10 NASB)

> The Lord is not slow in keeping his promise, as some understand slowness. He is patient with you, not wanting anyone to perish, but *everyone* to come to repentance (italics mine). (2 Peter 3:9 NIV)

> Jesus answered them, "It is not the healthy who need a doctor, but the sick. I have not come to call the righteous, but sinners to repentance." (Luke 5:31-32 NIV)

I could give you Scripture after Scripture about God's heart for lost people.[6] It's simple; Jesus loves lost people. It's the reason He came. You were that lost person once: alone, hurting, sinful, depressed, suicidal, selfish, crying out for help—and He loved you enough to come find you. He probably helped locate you through another person. Maybe this person invited you to church, shared the gospel with you, or prayed for you.

Regardless of how you came into relationship with Jesus, He cared about you enough to seek you out. He didn't wait until you had it together. He didn't simply send a book or a prophet. No, it was serious enough that He knew the only way people could be redeemed for the glory of His Father and for the salvation of their souls was for Him to leave heaven, come as a human being, live a perfect life, shed His blood on a rugged cross to pay for our sins, rise again from the dead, and conquer sin and death once and for all.

How can we not share the good news? It's too important. There is too much riding on it. It's more important than our fears and insecurities. It's more important than our reputation, the job we get, where we go to school, or what kind of car we drive. He showed us the way. Like Jesus, we need to dwell among people, living out our lives with God in front of the very ones we are trying to reach.

Luke 18:9-14 is one of my favorite passages concerning

the lost, or in all of Scripture for that matter. In the story, two men go to the Temple to pray, one a Pharisee and the other a tax collector (who were very despised in Jewish culture because they worked for the Romans and cheated people). The Pharisee prays a very arrogant prayer, saying, "God, I thank You that I am not like other men—extortioners, unjust, adulterers, or even as this tax collector. I fast twice a week; I give tithes of all I possess" (Luke 18:11-12). Can you see his smugness, his spiritual pride? He is basing his relationship with God on his performance!

Isaiah says is this way, "All of us have become like one who is unclean, and all our righteous acts are like filthy rags; we all shrivel up like a leaf, and like the wind our sins sweep us away" (Isa. 64:6 NIV). What right do we have to boast? We can't save ourselves. We couldn't even find God; He had to come find us! We were walking around poor, blind, naked, and wretched when He found us and lifted us out of our filth. Remember, "While we were yet sinners, Christ died for us" (Rom. 5:8).

The tax collector, on the other hand ,would not even look up to heaven, but instead stood at a distance and cried out in repentance, "God, have mercy on me a sinner" (Luke 18:13). Then Jesus says something profound about this man: "This man went home justified (free and innocent) before God. For everyone who exalts himself we be humbled and he who humbles himself will be exalted" (Luke 18:14). Like one of the criminals crucified with Jesus, this man found freedom! Jesus came to preach the gospel to the poor–those who were literally poor and those who were spiritually poor and understood their need for God. He is looking for people who will come to Him humbly. After all, if you're not lost, how can you be found?

Jesus' heart beats for the lost. "There's more rejoicing in heaven over one sinner who repents than over ninety-nine righteous persons who do not repent" (Luke 15:7). Let's pray and cry out for our lost friends and family members, and then at the appropriate time, show acts of kindness in Jesus' name, share the gospel with them, invite them to church, or take some type of action to ensure that they have opportunities to hear and obey the gospel. I love how pastor Perry Noble says it, "Found people find people!"[7]

Where would Jesus be if He was on your campus? He was

known to hang out with tax-collectors, prostitutes, and sinners. Would He be at a fraternity or a Finals Club? What room in your dorm would He hang out in? Who would He be reaching out to? We must be immersed in the culture while at the same time remaining holy. This can be a challenge, yet it is our calling. Our calling is not to cloister ourselves off into some religious community that's physically separate from the rest of humanity. That sounds more like a cult to me. Gather for times of refreshing and equipping with other believers, get filled up like in the book of Acts, and go turn the world upside down! I have some resources on how to share Christ with your lost friends in Appendix G. I also recommend you read the book called, *The Blueprint* by Jaeson Ma. It has some great tools on how to share Christ.

I still believe that relational evangelism (intentionally sharing Christ with those you have a relationship with or are building a relationship wtih) is the most effective way. Most people come to Christ through a friend or relative. That being said, I also believe that we aren't very good at it. This is evidenced by the fact that most followers of Jesus (at least in this country) have never led one person to Christ. Imagine if the estimated 50 million Christians in America led one person to Christ a year. Our nation would be won to Christ in only three years. It's awesome to invite a friend to church to hear the gospel; I'm not downing that, but what about those friends who will never darken the door of a church? How will they hear if they don't hear through you? You are God's chosen instrument to carry the Gospel to your friends and family.

I would encourage you to read a document I've put in Appendix H called, "That Hideous Doctrine." It's not meant to guilt you into anything, but only to help you think from the perspective of eternity. It may shock you, but more than that, I pray it will compel you to action. It vividly portrays the destiny that awaits those who don't know Christ.

As you go, remember Jesus is *always* with you. You can, no *you will,* make an impact for eternity. I will close with a quote from Amy Carmichael, a famous missionary to India: "We have moments to work, eternity to enjoy." Now *GO!*

Discussion Questions and Exercises

1. Write out your personal vision in a short, concise statement. If you don't know what it is, take an afternoon to seek God and let Him speak to you. Right now, schedule a date and tell a friend when you are going to do this.
2. Why do we exist? Why do you exist?
3. Restate the overflowing cup principle and answer this question honestly: Are you living with a full cup or an overflowing cup?
4. Does your heart reflect the same attitude that God's Word reflects about how much He loves lost people? If not, take time to meditate (read, mutter, chew on, think about) on Scriptures listed earlier in the chapter (Love for the Lost) and ask God to give you His heart for people. Ask that He would give you tears for your lost friends and family members.
5. What are you going to do about it? I have also included some resources in Appendix F and G to help you get started sharing Christ with your lost friends.

Resources

Appendix F: V.I.P. List by Kent Murawski
Appendix G: Resources for Evangelism by Kent Murawski
Appendix H: *That Hideous Doctrine* by John Thomas
The One Thing You Can't Do In Heaven by Mark Cahill
The Twelve Myths of Evangelism by Derek Levendusky
The Master Plan of Evangelism by Robert E. Coleman

Meditation Verse

Therefore, go and make disciples of all the nations, baptizing them in the name of the Father and the Son and the Holy Spirit. Teach these new disciples to obey all the commands I have given you. And be sure of this: I am with you always, even to the end of the age. (Matthew 28:19-20 NLT)

CONCLUSION

I pray this book has encouraged you and equipped you. Don't settle for a mediocre experience. Walk with God through high school and into college and young adult years. Pursue a vibrant, life-giving, passionate, and fruitful relationship with Christ. These are some of the greatest years of your life. Don't waste them!

ABOUT THE AUTHOR

Kent Murawski is a father, husband, author, and the lead pastor of Journey Church in Cambridge, MA (www.jcboston. org). Home to Harvard and MIT, Cambridge is like no other place on earth. It's an academic and political hotbed. To say Cambridge is influential is an understatement. Eight U.S. presidents have graduated from Harvard alone, and MIT boasts 81 Nobel laureates! Kent blogs extensively about leadership for the long haul (www.kentmurawski.com) and lives near Boston with his wife, Gina, and their three children. You can follow Kent on Twitter (@kentmurawski) and on Facebook at (www.fb.com/ kentmurawski).

CONTACT THE AUTHOR

I would love to hear from you. Have some input, a testimony, or a question?

Contact Kent:
Email: kentmurawski@gmail.com
Blog: www.kentmurawski.com
Twitter: @kentmurawski
Facebook: www.fb.com/kentmurawski
Sermons: www.jcboston.org/category/podcast
Journey Church: www.jcboston.org

Stay tuned for Kent's next book and subscribe to receive helpful input on leading for the long haul at www.kentmurawski.com!

APPENDIX A

Plan for "Devoted Time"

1. Worship/Thanksgiving (see John 4:23-24)
2. Bible Reading, study, meditation (see 2 Timothy 2:15)
3. Pray in the Spirit (see 1 Corinthians 14:18)
4. Prayer—asking, seeking, knocking, praying for others, and so forth (see Matthew 7:7)
5. Listening (Be Quiet!!!)—let God talk, follow promptings, impressions, thoughts, and so forth (see Psalms 46:10)

Notes

- Keep a journal
- Don't leave God in your devoted time! Learn to fellowship with Him throughout the day!
- Morning is the preferable time.
- Do each one for equal amount of minutes. Example: If your devoted time is one hour, do each one for 12 minutes.
- Don't be rigid! If you end up studying the Bible for the whole time one day, so be it!
- The main point is to connect with Jesus, so connect with Him!

APPENDIX B

Who I Am in Christ

Ephesians 1:3—I am complete in Christ; I have every spiritual blessing in Christ.

2 Peter 1:3—I have everything I need for living a godly life.

2 Corinthians 5:17—I am a new creation in Christ.

Ephesians 1:4—I was chosen before the foundation of the world to be holy and without blame in Christ.

Ephesians 1:5—God decided my adoption as a son or daughter in advance. All along, He had already formed me in His heart, designed me, picked me like the first pick on a team, created me, and birthed me according to the pleasure of His will. No one had to twist His arm or coax Him to do it; He wanted to. He chose me, created me, and wants me.

Ephesians 1:6—I am accepted and highly favored in Christ. I don't have to perform or act out to get His attention or approval; I already have it.

Psalm 17:8—I am the apple of His eye; when He looks at me, He has eyes only for me. Like a parent watching His child in a game, He sees the whole game, but focuses on me.

2 Peter 3:9—He is big enough and has enough room in His heart to focus on all His children. He has enough room in His heart for every person on the face of the earth, all those who have gone before us and all those yet to be created. His heart beats that all become His children and that none should perish in a life without purpose, apart from Him forever.

Ephesians 1:7—In Him I am free and have been delivered from my sins through His blood.

Ephesians 1:8—He lavished me with grace and wiped away my sin debt.

Psalm 103:3,12—I am completely forgiven; as far as the east is from the west, my sins have been removed from me. In fact, He has cast them into the depths of the sea and forgotten them (Micah 7:19).

Colossians 2:14—He cancelled the written record of charges against me and nailed it to the cross.

1 Corinthians 6:20—I have been bought with a price; I am no longer my own.

1 Peter 1:18-19—I have been purchased by the blood of the spotless lamb, Jesus Christ.

Ephesians 1:9—He let me in on His secrets about Christ. He only tells friends and confidants His secrets.

John 15:15—I am no longer a servant, but a friend of God.

Ephesians 1:13—I have been marked, sealed, and stamped by the Holy Spirit (or signed, sealed, and delivered, if you will). He is the promise of my inheritance to come. He is the guarantee of my inheritance in Christ. The Holy Spirit is how I know I have been destined to receive an inheritance in Christ.

Ephesians 1:19-20; 2:6; John 1:12-13—I am powerful in Christ. I have authority in Christ. I have explosive miraculous power in Christ.

Ephesians 2:6—I am seated with Christ in heavenly places. Because I am with Him, I am far above principalities and powers, might and dominion, and every name that is named in *this age and the one to come. I am identified by the name of Jesus, the name above all names.*

Ephesians 2:10—I have been created for good works, which God has laid out before the foundation of the world for me to walk in.

APPENDIX C

Keys to Freedom: Overcoming Sexual Addiction

These different keys in and of themselves will not deliver you from a sexual addiction, but what they will do is *position* you to receive freedom from God. They will put you in a place and posture of humility and brokenness and also allow you to keep your freedom once you gain it.

1. Freedom Key #1: *Admit* **you have a problem**

And no creature is hidden from his sight, but all are naked and exposed to the eyes of him to whom we must give account (Hebrews 4:13).

2. Freedom Key #2: You may need *deliverance!*

The Spirit of the Lord is upon me, because he hath anointed me to preach the gospel to the poor; he hath sent me to heal the brokenhearted, to preach deliverance to the captives, and recovering of sight to the blind, to set at liberty them that are bruised, To preach the acceptable year of the Lord (Luke 4:18-19).

- You must let God change your heart.
- John 8:32
- Freedom is yours for the taking—it's your right as a child of God, your inheritance!

3. Freedom Key #3: Get radical!

And if your hand or your foot causes you to sin, cut it off and throw it away. It is better for you to enter life crippled or lame than with two hands or two feet to be thrown into the eternal fire (Matthew 18:8).

- Turn off cable, cancel Internet, lose the boyfriend or girlfriend, and get help or counseling; sin leads to death!

4. Freedom Key #4: The power of confession

Therefore, confess your sins to one another and pray for one another, that you may be healed. The prayer of a righteous person has great power as it is working (James 5:16).

- Opening up your life (to the right person) may help you get free.

- Once you get free, you won't stay free without accountability. It's a tool, a weapon in your arsenal. There is something about taking something from the darkness of your heart and mind and exposing it to the light.

But if we walk in the light, as he is in the light, we have fellowship with one another, and the blood of Jesus his Son cleanses us from all sin (1 John 1:7).

- How can you be accountable to an invisible God if you can't be accountable to a visible person?
- Accountability only works if you have dealt with the issue and you can be honest with God and people. It doesn't help otherwise.

5. Freedom Key #5: Be committed to a local church

The righteous flourish like the palm tree and grow like a cedar in Lebanon. They are planted in the house of the LORD; they flourish in the courts of our God (Psalm 92:12-13).

6. Freedom Key #6: Continue to Grow

- You must continue to feed yourself biblical truth by putting the Scriptures in your heart, meditating, and reading material that helps you in this area.

I will hide your word in my heart that I might not sin against you (Psalm 119:11).

7. Freedom Key #7: Fasting and prayer

- Once you get victory, you must fight to keep it!

APPENDIX D

The Seven R's: Interceding for the 13/30 Generation

God gave me this verse and a picture of a teetering scale and said that my generation teeters in the balance. He also said, "It is intercessory prayer that will tip the balance in your favor."

> And I sought for a man among them who should build up the wall (hedge) and stand in the breach (gap) before me for the land, that I should not destroy it, but I found none. (Ezekiel 22:30)

The Seven R's

1. **Revelation**—Pray that our generation would have a *revelation* of who God is, the fear of the Lord, and God's holiness like Isaiah did in Isaiah chapter 6. Pray for the same response Isaiah had: "Here I am, send me."
2. **Revolution**—Pray that there would be a *revolution* of true worshipers who rise up among our generation (see John 4).
3. **Reputation**—Pray our generation would have a *reputation* as the generation that "seeks Your face, O God of Jacob" (see Psalm 24).
4. **Relationship**—Pray we would be known as the generation that values *relationship* with God above all else. It's no coincidence that our generation is craving relationship so much. I believe God set it up that way, but it's not only intended to be human relationship; it's also divine relationship. That's what "seeking His face" is all about (see John 15).
5. **Repentance**—Pray that our generation would experience godly sorrow that leads to true *repentance* (see 2 Cor. 7:10).
6. **Restoration**—Pray that our generation would be *restored* to

a right standing with God and that we would cry out for the lost (see 1 John 2:2).

7. **Revival**—Pray that our generation would taste, see, and experience the results of authentic *revival*—repentance and a healing of our land (see 2 Chron. 7:14).

APPENDIX E

Sample Monthly Budget   Month:_____

Monthly Expenses	Amount	Paid	Notes
Tithe	_____	_____	_____
Offering	_____	_____	_____
Offering	_____	_____	_____
Car Insurance	_____	_____	_____
Gas & Oil	_____	_____	_____
Car Maint.	_____	_____	_____
Life Ins.	_____	_____	_____
Mortgage/Rent	_____	_____	_____
Cleaning Supplies	_____	_____	_____
Groceries	_____	_____	_____
Electric	_____	_____	_____
Heat	_____	_____	_____
Phone	_____	_____	_____
Cable	_____	_____	_____
Internet	_____	_____	_____
House	_____	_____	_____
Credit Card	_____	_____	_____
Car Loan	_____	_____	_____
Additional Debt	_____	_____	_____
Savings	_____	_____	_____
Emergency Fund	_____	_____	_____
Other	_____	_____	_____
Doctor	_____	_____	_____
Dentist	_____	_____	_____
Entertainment	_____	_____	_____
Eat out	_____	_____	_____
Personal Items	_____	_____	_____
Clothes	_____	_____	_____
Hair	_____	_____	_____
Misc.	_____	_____	_____
Stamps	_____	_____	_____
Gifts	_____	_____	_____
Municipal water	_____	_____	_____
Garbage	_____	_____	_____
	_____	_____	_____
	_____	_____	_____

Totals Spent (column #1): _____

Net Income: _____

Surplus: _____

Monthly Income:

	Gross Pay:		Net Pay:
Check #1	_____	Check #1	_____
Check #2	_____	Check #2	_____
Check #3	_____	Check #3	_____
Check #4	_____	Check #4	_____
Other	_____	Other	_____
Total Gross:	_____	Total Net:	_____

Tithe (from gross) _____
Total Net Monies For the Month: _____
Total Expenses For the Month: _____
Surplus For Month: _____

APPENDIX F

V.I.P. List

Adapted from Weiner Ministries Intl. (www.youthnow.org)

> The Lord is not slow in keeping his promise, as some understand slowness. He is patient with you, not wanting anyone to perish, but everyone to come to repentance. (2 Peter 3:9 NIV)

1._____

2._____

3._____

4._____

5._____

6._____

*Use this list to write down, consistently pray for, and share the gospel with these people (and/or invite them to church). You could sum it up by saying, "Pray, Care, and Share."

APPENDIX G

Resources for Evangelism
Praying for Those Far From God

- Use V.I.P. List
- Pray five minutes per day
- Name them individually
- Ask God to send laborers (including you) to them (see Luke 10:1-2). Set your cell phone alarm for 10:02 every day and pray for laborers when it rings.
- Pray that the light of the gospel would shine on them (see 2 Cor. 4:3-4).
- Pray that the Holy Spirit would soften their hearts and make them good ground to receive the seed of God's Word (see Matt. 13:23).

Relational Evangelism

- Pray for those in your circle of friends and acquaintances.
- Develop the relationship! Be intentional and at some point steer the conversation in a spiritual direction.
- Be transparent and real. Nobody likes a fake.
- Step out! Share the gospel and invite people to church (see Rom. 10:13-14).
- Do your part and leave the rest in God's hands (see 1 Cor. 3:6-7).

Ways of Sharing the Gospel

- The Romans Road—Romans 3:23; 6:23; 1 Thess. 1:8-9; Romans 10:9-10
- Using the 10 Commandments—Exodus 20:1-17, http://www.livingwaters.com/
- Four Spiritual Laws—http://www.campuscrusade.com/fourlawseng.htm
- Basic elements—Matt. 1:23; Heb. 4:15; Rom. 5:8; 1 Cor. 15:4, 54-57
- Billy Graham Tracts - http://www.billygrahambookstore.org/product.asp?sku=2161_82134P25

APPENDIX H

That Hideous Doctrine

by John Thomas

That hideous doctrine of hell is fading. How often have you thought of it in the last month, for instance? Does it make a difference in your concern for others, in your witness? Is it a constant and proper burden? Most believers would have to say no. But the individual isn't the only one to blame. After all, the doctrine no longer gets its float in the church parade; it has become a museum piece at best, stored in the shadows of a far corner.

The reality of hell, however, demands we haul the monstrous thing out again and study it until it changes us. Ugly, garish, and familiar as it is, this doctrine will indeed have a daily, practical, and personal effect on every believer who comes to terms with its force.

Our Lord's words on the subject are unnerving. In Luke 16, He tells us of a rich man who died and went to Hades (the abode of the unsaved between death and final judgment). From that story and a few other revelatory facts, we can infer several characteristics of hell.

First, it's a place of *great physical pain*. The rich man's initial remark concludes with his most pressing concern: "I am in agony in this flame" (Luke 16:24). We do not make enough of this. We have all experienced pain to some degree. We know it can make a mockery of all life's goals and beauties. Yet we do not seem to know pain as a hint of hell, a searing foretaste of what will befall those who do not know Christ, a grim reminder of what we will be spared from.

God does not leave us with simply the mute fact of hell's physical pain. He tells us how real people will react to that pain. Our Lord is not being macabre; He is simply telling us the truth.

First, there will be *"weeping"* (Luke 13:28). Weeping is not something we get a grip on; it is something that grips us. Recall how you were affected when you last heard someone weep. Remember how you were moved with compassion to want to protect and restore that person? The Lord wants us to know and consider what an upsetting experience it is for the person in hell.

Another response will be *"wailing"* (Matthew 13:42). While weeping attracts our sympathy, wailing frightens and offends us. It is the pitiable bawl of a soul seeking escape, hurt beyond repair, eternally damaged. A wail is sound gone grotesque because of conclusions we can't live with.

A third response will be *"gnashing of teeth"* (Luke 13:28). Why? Perhaps because of anger or frustration. It may be a defense against crying out or an intense pause when one is too weary to cry any longer.

Hell has two other aspects, rarely considered, which are both curious and frightening. On earth we take for granted two physical properties that keep us physically, mentally, and emotionally stable. The first is light; the second is solid, fixed surfaces. Oddly, these two dependable will not accommodate those in hell.

Hell is a *place of darkness* (Matthew 8:12). Imagine the person who has just entered hell—a neighbor, relative, co-worker, or friend. After a roar of physical pain blasts him, he spends his first few moments wailing and gnashing his teeth. But after a season, he grows accustomed to the pain, not that it's become tolerable, but that his capacity for it has enlarged to comprehend it, yet not be consumed by it. Though he hurts, he is now able to think, and he instinctively looks about him. But as he looks, he sees only blackness.

In his past life he learned that if he looked long enough, a glow of light somewhere would yield definition to his surroundings. So he blinks and strains to focus his eyes, but his efforts yield only blackness. He turns and strains his eyes in another direction. He waits. He sees nothing but unyielding black ink. It clings to him, smothering and oppressing him.

Realizing that the darkness is not going to give way, he nervously begins to feel for something solid to get his bearings. He reaches for walls or rocks or trees or chairs; he stretches his legs to feel the ground and touches nothing.

Hell is a *"bottomless pit"* (Revelation 20:1-2, KJV); however, the new occupant is slow to learn. In growing pain, he kicks his feet and waves his arms. He stretches and lunges. But he finds nothing. After more feverish tries, he pauses from exhaustion, suspended in black. Suddenly, with a scream he kicks, twists, and lunges until he is again too exhausted to move.

He hangs there, alone with his pain. Unable to touch a solid object or see a solitary thing, he begins to weep. His sobs choke through the darkness. They become weak, lost in hell's roar.

As time passes, he begins to do what the rich man did—he again starts to think. His first thoughts are of hope. You see, he still thinks as he did on earth, where he kept himself alive with hope. When things got bad, he always found a way out. If he felt pain, he took medicine. If he were hungry, he ate food. If he lost love, there was always more love to be found.

So he casts about his mind for a plan to apply to the hope building in his chest. "Of course," he thinks. "Jesus, the God of love, can get me out of this." He cries out with a surge, "Jesus! Jesus! I believe now! Save me from this!" Again the darkness smothers his words.

Our sinner is not unique. Everyone in hell believes (James 2:19).

When he wearies of appeals, he does next what anyone would do—assess his situation and attempts to adapt. But then it hits him—*This is forever.* Jesus made it very clear. He used the same words for "forever" to describe both heaven and hell.

"Forever," he thinks, and his mind labors through the blackness until he aches. "Forever!" he whispers in wonder. The idea deepens, widens, and towers over him.

The awful truth spreads before him like endless, overlapping slats: "When I put in ten thousands centuries of time here, I will not have accomplished one thing. I will not have one second less to spend here."

As the rich man pleaded for a drop of water, so, too, our new occupant entertains a similar ambition. In life he learned that even bad things could be tolerated if one could find temporary relief. Perhaps even hell, if one could rest from time to time, would be tolerable.

He learns, though, that "the smoke of [his] torment goes up for ever and ever; and [he has] no rest, day or night" (Revelation 14:11).

No rest day and night—think of that.

Thoughts of this happening to people we know; people like us, are too terrifying to entertain for long. The idea of allowing someone to endure such torture for eternity violates the sensibilities of even the most sever judge among us. We simply cannot bear it.

But our thoughts of hell will never be as unmanageable as its reality. We must take this doctrine of hell, therefore, and make sure we are practically affected by it.

A hard look at this doctrine should first change our view of sin. Most believers do not take sin as seriously as God does. We need to realize that in God's eyes, and in His actual plan, sin deserves eternal punishment in hell. We actually learn, by comparison, to hate sin as God hates it. As the reality of hell violates and offends us, for example, so sin violates and offends God. As we cannot bear to look upon the horrors of hell, so God cannot bear to look upon the horrors of sin. As hell revolts us to the point of hatred for it, so God finds sin revolting. The comparison is not perfect, but it offers a start. Second, the truth of hell should encourage our witness. Can we ever hear a sigh of weariness, see a moment of doubt, or feel pain without being reminded of that place? In all honesty, can we see any unbeliever, watch his petty human activities, realize what he has in store, and not be moved with compassion? It encourages us to witness in word and in deed.

That hideous doctrine may grip our souls in dark terror and make us weep, but let us be sure it also prompts us to holiness and compassion.[1]

APPENDIX I

A Note to Parents and Leaders

Parents

You are the most important influence in the life of your children. I pray this book will help you to navigate these years with your children and talk about these issues with them. It's never too late to start a relationship with your kids. If you haven't done it, it may take some time, but it's worth the investment! Why not go through this book with them. It will bring up some good opportunities to talk to them about different issues. Or possibly consider taking a group of young people through the book. Depending on your relationship with your son or daughter, they may not want to talk about some of these issues in front of you, but you could always go through the book alone and encourage them if this is the case. Regardless of how you do it, it would be good for you to read and study this book to know and understand better some of the issues they are facing.

Leaders

As a youth worker and a youth pastor for five years, and currently as a lead pastor, I know the investment you make in children and teenagers. I also know you don't make that investment with the hope that you will lose three out of four of them when they graduate high school. *We simply can't lead with the mentality of getting them through high school. We must lead with the conviction that we are going to help equip them to thrive through these critical years.* I'm not saying we have to visit them every weekend at college, but I am saying we must come up with an intentional strategy to stop the growing exodus of church kids who are leaving the ranks shortly after they graduate.

APPENDIX J

How to Use in a Small Group Setting

This book was written with small groups in mind. The topics are such that they are better dealt with in the context of community. At the end of each chapter, there are discussion questions that are meant to get to the heart of the issue. Each week a chapter or chapters are read and the discussion questions are answered. The group should then meet on a weekly basis to discuss the chapter(s) and discussion questions and to pray for one another. Here is a breakdown of how the chapters can be studied:

Week 1 – Introduction
Week 2 – Chapters 1 and 2
Week 3 – Chapter 3 and 4
Week 4 – Chapter 5 and 6
Week 5 – Chapters 7 and 8
Week 6 – Chapter 9 and 10
Week 7 – Chapters 11 and 12
Week 8 – Chapter 13 and 14
Week 9 – Chapter 15 and 16
Week 10 – Catch up week
Weeks 11 – Party week

If you wish to carry it out another week, that is possible. Also, it is possible to focus on certain key chapters you think are the most relevant, making it an 8-week small group.

ENDNOTES

Chapter 1: My Story

[1] J. Edwin Orr, "The Role of Prayer in Spiritual Awakening," October 1976, speech, Garland, TX. Excerpt cited in "Conditions That Require Revival," Revival Library, accessed December 16, 2013. http://www.revival-library.org/index.php/resources-menu/revival-anecdotes/conditions-that-require-revival.

[2] Orr, "The Role of Prayer in Spiritual Awakening."

[3] Michael F. Gleason, When God Walked On Campus, (Joshua Press, 2002), 27. Quoting Benjamin Rice Lacy, Jr. Revivals in the Midst of the Years, 1943 ed. (Hopewell, VA: Royal Publishers, Inc., 1968), 70.

[4] Gleason, When God Walked On Campus

[5] Gleason, When God Walked On Campus

[6] Dr. Charles Habib-Malik was a renowned scholar, international diplomat, and the thirteenth President of the UN General Council.

[7] Gleason, When God Walked on Campus, 29.

[8] Gleason, When God Walked On Campus, 26.

[9] Gregory A. Smith, "Adoniram Judson," Baptist Bible Tribune, accessed January 7, 2014, http://www.tribune.org/adoniram-judson/.

[10] Dennis Gaylor, Reach the U: A Handbook for Effective College Ministry, (Springfield, MO: Chi Alpha Campus Ministries, 2003), 81. Taken from Schmidt, Alvin J., Under the Influence: How Christianity Transformed Civilization, (Grand Rapids, MI: Zondervan, 2001).

[11] "History of the Harvard Presidency," Harvard University, accessed January 7, 2014, http://www.harvard.edu/history-presidency.

[13] "The Vision," Justice House of Prayer Boston, accessed January 13, 2014, http://jhopboston.com/vision.

[14] "National University Rankings," U.S. News and World Report, accessed January 13, 2014, http://colleges.usnews.rankingsandreviews.com/best-colleges/rankings/national-universities.

[15] Campus Renewal Ministries, accessed 2008, http://www.campusrenewal.org, This paragraph was from their old website which is no longer in existence.

[16] Andy Stanley, Lane Jones, and Reggie Joiner, Seven Practices of Effective Ministry, (Colorado Springs, CO: Multnomah Books, 2008), 143.

[17] "Most Twentysomethings Put Christianity on the Shelf Following Spiritually Active Teen Years," Barna Group, September 11, 2006, accessed September 20, 2016, https://www.barna.com/research/most-twentysomethings-put-christianity-on-the-shelf-following-spiritually-active-teen-years/#.V-GtU2Vbo69.

[18] "Five Myths about Young Adult Church Dropouts," Barna Group, November 16, 2011, accessed September 20, 2016, https://www.barna.com/research/five-myths-about-young-adult-church-dropouts/#.V-GuCGVbo69.

[19] Scott McConnell, "Lifeway Research Finds Reasons 18-to-22-Year-Olds Drop Out of Church," Lifeway, August 7, 2007, accessed September 20, 2016, http://www.lifeway.com/Article/LifeWay-Research-finds-reasons-18-to-22-year-olds-drop-out-of-church.

[20] "Six Reasons Young Christians Leave Church," Barna Group, September 27, 2011, accessed September 20, 2016, https://www.barna.com/research/six-reasons-young-christians-leave-church/#.V-GvamVbo69.

[21] "Six Reasons Young Christians Leave Church."

[22] Apollo 13, directed by Ron Howard (Universal City, CA: Universal Studios, 1995.) Originally said by John Swigert, Jr. of the Apollo 13 moon flight to report

an electrical problem, and later used as the tagline for the film.

[23] Adam Clarke, Adam Clarke's Commentary on the Bible, abridged by Ralph Earl, (Kansas City, MO: Beacon Hill Press of Kansas City, 1967).

[24] Dale Schlafer, Revival 101: Understanding How Christ Ignites His Church, (Colorado Springs, CO: NavPress, 2003), 21.

[25] Lillian Kwon, "Total U.S. Churches No Longer in Decline, Researchers Say," The Christian Post, May 13, 2010, accessed September 20, 2016, http://www.christianpost.com/news/total-us-churches-no-longer-in-decline-researchers-say-45150/.

[25] Lillian Kwon, "Total U.S. Churches No Longer in Decline, Researchers Say," The Christian Post, May 13, 2010, accessed September 20, 2016, http://www.christianpost.com/news/total-us-churches-no-longer-in-decline-researchers-say-45150/.

Chapter 2: Do It Again, Lord

[1] Referring to the church bells that would ring during my noon-time class. This poem was written in that class in 1995.

[2] Merriam-Webster OnLine, s.v. "clairvoyant," accessed September 14, 2016. http://www.merriam-webster.com/dictionary/clairvoyant.

Chapter 3: Understanding the Basics

[1] WordNet, s.v. "apologetics," accessed February 19, 2014, http://wordnetweb.princeton.edu/perl/webwn?s-apologetics.

[2] C. J. Mahaney and Kevin Meath, The Cross Centered Life, (Colorado Springs, CO: Multnomah Books, 2002), 31.

[3] Mahaney and Meath, The Cross Centered Life, 31.

[4] Derek Levendusky, Discipleship By Grace, (Potter, KS: International Localization Network, 2010), 33.

[5] Mother Elizabeth Dabney, "Seeking God Until It Hurts," Charisma Magazine, November 29, 2012, accessed March 4, 2014, http://www.charismamag.com/spirit/prayer/2388-praying-through.

[6] Levendusky, Discipleship By Grace, 30.

Chapter 4: Abiding In Christ

[1] Bruce Wilkinson, Secrets of the Vine, (Colorado Springs, CO: Multnomah Publishers, 2001), 21.

[2] Wilkinson, Secrets of the Vine, 34-35.

[3] Wilkinson, Secrets of the Vine, 65.

[4] "G3306 - menō - Strong's Greek Lexicon (NKJV)." Blue Letter Bible. Accessed 14 September, 2016. https://www.blueletterbible.org//lang/lexicon/lexicon.cfm?Strongs=G3306&t=NKJV

[5] John Piper, interview, "What Is God's Glory," Ask Pastor John, Desiring God, July 6, 2009, http://www.desiringgod.org/interviews/what-is-gods-glory.

Chapter 5: The Father Heart of God

[1] Mac Anderson and Lance Wubbels, To Love a Child Is Spelled T-I-M-E:

What A Child Really Needs from You (Nashville: FaithWords, 2004), 12-13.
    [2] "Statistics." The Fatherless Generation, accessed September 10, 2014, http://thefatherlessgeneration.wordpress.com/statistics.
    [3] Walk the Line, directed by James Mangold (Los Angeles, CA: 20th Century Fox, 2005).
    [4] Leonard Ravenhill, Why Revival Tarries, (CITY OF PUBLICATION: Bethany House, 2004), PAGE NUMBER.

Chapter 6: The Spirit of Adoption

    [1] "G71 - agō - Strong's Greek Lexicon (KJV)." Blue Letter Bible. Accessed 14 September, 2016. https://www.blueletterbible.org//lang/lexicon/lexicon.cfm?Strongs=G71&t=KJV.
    [2] Easton, Matthew George. "Entry for Adoption." Easton's Bible Dictionary, accessed September 20, 2016, http://www.biblestudytools.com/dictionaries/eastons-bible-dictionary/adoption.html.
    [3] Dutch Sheets, Roll Away Your Stone: Living in the Power of the Risen Christ (Minneapolis, MN: Bethany House, 2007), 99.
    [4] Clarke, Adam. "Commentary on Romans 8:4" The Adam Clarke Commentary, accessed September 16, 2016, www.studylight.org/commentaries/acc/romans-8.html.

Chapter 7: Know Thyself

    [1] "G602 - apokalypsis - Strong's Greek Lexicon (KJV)." Blue Letter Bible. Accessed 14 September, 2016. https://www.blueletterbible.org//lang/lexicon/lexicon.cfm?Strongs=G602&t=KJV.
    [2] The Matrix, directed by The Wachowski Brothers (Burbank, CA: Warner Bros, 1999).

Chapter 8: Rooted and Planted

    [1] T. Rees, "Choose; Chosen," in The International Standard Bible Encyclopedia, vol 1, ed G. W. Bromiley, (Grand Rapids, MI: Wm B. Eerdmans, 1979-1988), 693.
    [2] Barnes, Albert. "Commentary on Matthew 16:4" Barnes' Notes on the New Testament, accessed September 20, 2016, www.studylight.org/commentaries/bnb/matthew-16.html.
    [3] G. W. Bromiley, "Church," in The International Standard Bible Encyclopedia, vol 1, (Grand Rapids, MI: Wm B. Eerdmans, 1979-1988), 693.
    [4] Bromiley, "Church," 693.
    [5] "G2842 - koinōnia - Strong's Greek Lexicon (KJV)." Blue Letter Bible. Accessed 14 September, 2016. https://www.blueletterbible.org//lang/lexicon/lexicon.cfm?Strongs=G2842&t=KJV.
    [6] C. J. Mahaney, Why Small Groups, (Gaithersburg, MD: Sovereign Grace Ministries, 1996), 18.
    [7] Mahaney, Why Small Groups, 19.
    [8] Barnes, Albert. "Commentary on Acts 2:42," Barnes' Notes on the New Testament, accessed September 20, 2016, www.studylight.org/commentaries/bnb/acts-2.html.
    [9] The Lord of the Rings: The Return of the King, directed by Peter Jackson (Los Angeles, CA: New Line Cineman, 2003).

[10] adapted from Mark Driscoll, "What is the Church," Vimeo video, 1:05:55, from a sermon given at Vintage Church, Santa Monica, CA, uploaded June 15, 2009, accessed September 20, 2016, https://vimeo.com/5170861.

Chapter 9: Overcoming Sexual Temptation

[1] Rob Jackson, "When Children View Pornography," Focus on the Family, accessed February 24, 2015, http://www.focusonthefamily.com/lifechallenges/love-and-sex/pornography/how-to-confront-children-using-pornography.

[2] "Pornography Statistics," Family Safe Media, accessed February 24, 2015, http://www.familysafemedia.com/pornography_statistics.html.

[3] Sharon Jayson, "Teens Define Sex in New Ways," USA Today, October 19, 2005, accessed September 14, 2016, http://usatoday30.usatoday.com/news/health/2005-10-18-teens-sex_x.htm.

[4] "H3063 - Yĕhuwdah - Strong's Hebrew Lexicon (KJV)." Blue Letter Bible. Accessed 14 September, 2016. https://www.blueletterbible.org//lang/lexicon/lexicon.cfm?Strongs=H3063&t=KJV.

[5] K. G. Jung, "Baal." In The International Standard Bible Encyclopedia, vol 1, ed. G. W. Bromiley, (Grand Rapids, MI: Wm B. Eerdmans, 1988), 377.

[6] Chuck Pierce and Dutch Sheets, "Prayer Warriors: Rise Up Against the Strongmen in this Nation," The Elijah List, March 8, 2007, accessed September 14, 2016, http://www.elijahlist.com/words/display_word/5068.

[7] Douglass Weiss, The Final Freedom, (Colorado Springs, CO: Discovery Press, 2008).

[8] "Pornography Statistics."

[9] "Ted Haggard Talks," Oprah Winfrey, June 30, 2009, accessed March 31, 2015, http://www.oprah.com/oprahshow/Ted-Haggard-and-His-Wife-Talk-About-the-Gay-Sex-Scandal.

[10] Bruce Wilkinson, Experiencing Spiritual Breakthroughs, (Colorado Springs, CO: Multnomah Books, 1999), 110-111.

[11] "What Are Endorphins?" from The Road to Health (blog), accessed September 20, 2016, http://www.road-to-health.com/64/What_are_Endorphins_.html.

[12] "Statistics on Pornography, DATE LAST MODIFIED, Sexual Addiction, and Online Perpetrators," Safe Families, accessed April 29, 2015, http://www.safefamilies.org/sfStats.php.

Chapter 10: Choosing the Right Relationships

[1] H. Jackson Brown, Jr. "21 Suggestions for Success" 21 Suggestions, accessed June 24, 2015, http://www.21suggestions.com.

[2] "H5048 - neged - Strong's Hebrew Lexicon (KJV)." Blue Letter Bible. Accessed 14 September, 2016. https://www.blueletterbible.org//lang/lexicon/lexicon.cfm?Strongs=H5048&t=KJV

[3] John Gill, "Deuteronomy 22:10," John Gill's Exposition of the Bible, on Bible Study Tools, accessed September 20, 2016, http://www.biblestudytools.com/commentaries/gills-exposition-of-the-bible/deuteronomy-22-10.html.

[4] Clarke, Adam. "Commentary on 2 Corinthians 6:4," The Adam Clarke Commentary, accessed September 20, 2016, www.studylight.org/commentaries/acc/2-corinthians-6.html.

[5] "Sociological Reasons Not to Live Together," last modified December 8, 2008, All About Cohabiting Before Marriage, accessed May 11, 2015, http://www.leaderu.com/critical/cohabitation-socio.html.

Chapter 11: Making Good Decisions

[1] Mike Cavanaugh was the pastor of Elim Gospel Church in Lima, NY for 20 years and now serves as the Vice President of Elim Fellowship and the President of Elim Bible Institute, www.elimfellowship.org and www.elim.edu.

[2] "H3513 - kabad - Strong's Hebrew Lexicon (NKJV)." Blue Letter Bible. Accessed 14 September, 2016. https://www.blueletterbible.org//lang/lexicon/lexicon.cfm?Strongs=H3513&t=NKJV.

[3] John Maxwell, "Seven Principles of Planning," Team Expansion, accessed June 1, 2015, http://www.teamexpansion.org/brigguy/articles/Seven_Principles_of_Planning.pdf

[4] The pastor I'm referring to is, again, Mike Cavanaugh, the one who taught me the four things to consider when making a decision.

[5] Walt Henrichsen quote from Steve Shadrach, The Fuel and the Flame (Waynesboro, GA: Authentic Lifestyle, 2003), 77.

[6] Shadrach, The Fuel and the Flame, 74.

[7] Stanley, Joiner, and Jones, Seven Practices of Effective Ministry, 143.

Chapter 12: Defending Your Faith

[1] Mark Batterson, Primal: A Quest for the Lost Soul of Christianity, (Colorado Springs, CO: Multnomah Books, 2009), 6.

[2] "Intellectualism," The Basics of Philosophy, accessed September 20, 2016, http://www.philosophybasics.com/branch_intellectualism.html.

[3] "G3339 - metamorphoō - Strong's Greek Lexicon (NKJV)." Blue Letter Bible. Accessed 15 September, 2016. https://www.blueletterbible.org//lang/lexicon/lexicon.cfm?Strongs=G3339&t=NKJV

[4] "Transformation," Dictionary.com. Dictionary.com Unabridged. Random House, Inc., accessed September 28, 2016, http://www.dictionary.com/browse/transformation.

[5] "Renovate," Dictionary.com. Dictionary.com Unabridged. Random House, Inc., accessed September 28, 2016, http://www.dictionary.com/browse/renovate.

[6] Mark Batterson, "Holy Resolution," January 24, 2011, accessed June 24, 2015, http://www.markbatterson.com/uncategorized/holy-resolution/

Chapter 13: Money Management

[1] Randy Alcorn, The Treasure Principle, (Sisters, OR: Multnomah Publishers, 2001), 8.

[2] Rev. Ed Herd, "R. G. LeTourneau: Model of Generosity," accessed July 27, 2015, http://www3.telus.net/st_simons/nsnews019.html.

[3] Dictionary.com s.v. "steward," accessed September 14, 2016, http://www.dictionary.com/browse/steward?s=t.

[4] Schlafer, Revival 101.

[5] "H1061 - bikkuwr - Strong's Hebrew Lexicon (NKJV)." Blue Letter Bible. Accessed 15 September, 2016. https://www.blueletterbible.org//lang/lexicon/lexicon.cfm?Strongs=H1061&t=NKJV

[6] "H779 - 'arar - Strong's Hebrew Lexicon (NKJV)." Blue Letter Bible. Accessed 15 September, 2016. https://www.blueletterbible.org//lang/lexicon/lexicon.cfm?Strongs=H779&t=NKJV

[7] Steps #1, 2, and 7 are Kent's.

Chapter 14: You Need Power

[1] "G3306 - menō - Strong's Greek Lexicon (NKJV)."

[2] David Pawson, Word and Spirit Together, Kindle edition (Bradford-on-Avon, UK: Terra Nova Publications, 2007), 545.

[3] "G1411 - dynamis - Strong's Greek Lexicon (NKJV)." Blue Letter Bible. Accessed 15 September, 2016. https://www.blueletterbible.org//lang/lexicon/lexicon.cfm?Strongs=G1411&t=NKJV

[4] Peter Haas, The Skeptic's Guide to Tongues and Prophecy, accessed September 14, 2016, http://www.peterhaas.org/wp-content/uploads/2015/04/SkepticsGuideToTongues2015.pdf

Chapter 15: Finding Your Purpose

[1] "G4282 - proetoimazō - Strong's Greek Lexicon (NKJV)." Blue Letter Bible. Accessed 15 September, 2016. https://www.blueletterbible.org//lang/lexicon/lexicon.cfm?Strongs=G4282&t=NKJV

[2] Joshua Finley, "One Thing I Do When I'm Anxious and Overwhelmed," Joshua Finley Blog, July 9 2014, accessed October 13, 2015, http://joshuafinley.org/2014/07/09/one-thing-i-do-when-im-feeling-anxious-and-overwhelmed/

Chapter 16: GO

[1] John Piper, "Christian Hedonism: Forgive the Label, But Don't Miss the Truth," Desiring God Blog, January 1, 1995, accessed October 14, 2015. http://www.desiringgod.org/articles/christian-hedonism.

[2] "Habit 2: Begin With the End in Mind," , Stephen R Covey, accessed September 14, 2016, https://www.stephencovey.com/7habits/7habits-habit2.php.

[3] R. Jamieson, A. R. Fausset, and D. Brown, "Habakkuk 2:2." In Commentary Critical and Explanatory on the Whole Bible, (Oak Harbor, WA: Logos Research Systems, Inc., 1997) PAGE NUMBER.

[4] Ted Haggard – I personally heard him say this in a sermon

[5] Pastor Rick Bezet of New Life Church in Arkansas said this during a church planters training. You can read more about him at https://www.newlifechurch.tv/

[6] Matt. 9:9-13, Luke 5:31-32, Luke 15:1-10, Luke 18:9-14, Luke 19:10, John 3:16-19, 1 Tim. 1:15, 2 Peter 3:9

[7] Perry Noble, "Day #1 - Found People Find People," Perry Noble Blog, May 12, 2012, accessed October 26, 2015, https://perrynoble.com/blog/day-1-found-people-find-people.

Appendix

[1] John Thomas, "That Hideous Doctrine," *Moody Monthly*, September 1985. Reprinted with permission from Moody Publishers.

NOTES

NOTES

NOTES

NOTES

NOTES

NOTES

37006338R00158

Made in the USA
Middletown, DE
16 November 2016